Making Merry

Clare Bevan

www.newgeneration-publishing.com

 New Generation Publishing

INTRODUCTION

****

From Clare Bevan.

'MAKING MERRY.'

Dear Christmas Readers

Now here at last is: 'Making Merry'. (Part Two.)

So now you'll find some last minute presents; a festive folk-song; the Spirit Of Christmas; a joyful Christmas Play; memories of our late Queen; a splendid spread; more Santa sagas; Boxing Day blues; and many Good Intentions.

So curl up in a cosy chair and have fun!

****

'They've given me soap and talc again,
And bubble bath and scent -
I'm sure they didn't mean to be rude
I'm sure it was kindly meant.

It could all be coincidental,
It's very hard to tell -
But tonight I'm going to use the lot...
And tomorrow - I'll really SMELL!

****

Dedication,

For Martin, for everything!

****

A BIG CHRISTMAS 'THANK YOU' PAGE.

****

First:
An enormous thank you to all my wonderful Readers.
The lovely Bracknell Drama Club Crew who have always read my poems so splendidly - plus special thanks to Ann and Roger, who turned my little Christmas collections into jolly-holly booklets.
All our brilliant Musicians, especially: Bea, John, Tim and Kim.
All the brave children who sang along and enjoyed the fun!
And of course, dear old Ted who knew Father Christmas so well.

****

Second:
All the friends and fans who have come along to our 'Poems and Pies' shows.
Some of you have been to EVERY show since 1985! And now our new audiences and readers in friendly Crowthorne.
You have helped us raise a great deal of money for our local families, who are coping with Muscular Dystrophy - thank you SO much.

****

Third:
Our 'Poems and Pies' friends from all over the country:
Axmouth; Canterbury; Ian Tracey and Readers from Liverpool Cathedral; Stockport; The Wirral; Orkney; London; Croydon; Stowupland, Henley and more.

****

Fourth

Famous Friends - especially Sir Richard Baker, who used my poems at the Barbican and on B.B.C. Radio Four - and gave me some merry ideas.

Dear Sir Ken Dodd and Lady Anne Dodd, who inspired so many of my favourite poems. Ken's festive voice is on our Answer Phone - so he can still give me a nudge when it's time to start a new set of cheery poems.

****

And finally, Martin and Ben - who have not only performed their poems brilliantly, but have also put out the chairs for the audience...and cleared up afterwards!
(More importantly, Martin is now our contact with good old Santa Claus!)

THANK YOU ALL.
****

(And if this book sells well, some of my profits will go to Muscular Dystrophy U.K.)

v

CONTENTS:

****

1. A MERRY MARKET.

****

****

2. THE SPIRIT OF CHRISTMAS.

****

****

3. MAKING MERRY.

****

****

4. A FESTIVE FEAST.

****

****

5. MORE SANTA - SAGAS.

****

****

6. BOXING DAY AND AFTER !

****

****

7. GOOD INTENTIONS.

****

****

****

A MERRY MARKET.

****

A MERRY MARKET.

****

Roll up now ! Roll up
For the Big Christmas Fair -
It's famous. It's festive.
It's everywhere.

There are clowns on stilts. There are smoky smells.
There are hoop-la games. There are wishing wells.
There's the bim-bam-boom of the Oompah- Band.
There are shiny gifts that are made by hand:
There's a Rudolph Nose, or a Snowman Cake,
Or a Magic Box - or a Toy to make.
You begin to spend, though you don't know why -
There's a runny cheese that you have to try.
There are bargain sweets at a bargain price;
There's a cup of wine with a dose of spice;
There are chestnuts (black). There are garlands (red).
There's a Reindeer (old) in a painted shed.
There's a Grotto (small). There's an Elf (bright blue).
There's a Santa (plump). There's a frozen queue.
Yet although the Fair seems a waste of time,
When the children sing. When the handbells chime.
When the crowds look up
At a silver star.
Are you glad you came ?
Yes, of course you are.

Roll up now ! Roll up for the Big Christmas Fair.
It's famous. It's festive.
EVERYWHERE.

****

2

THE CHRISTMAS ADVERTS.

****

Here come the Adverts -
It's early November,
Our Hallowe'en pumpkin is losing its splendour...
And suddenly there !
On the T.V. screen,
Christmas trees sparkle and Santas are seen.

The snow-scenes are charming
Since no one seems chilly,
Their jumpers are jolly, their fashions are frilly;
The dancers are skipping
Down glittery stairs
To show us their lovely new tables and chairs.

The meals make us dribble -
A wise Fairy buys
A glossy great turkey, a mound of mince-pies.
And sumptuous cakes
Which are bargains SO cheap
No one will ever lose money. Or sleep.

Elves juggle gadgets
We simply MUST buy.
Cute little children bring tears to the eye -
A heart-rending lyric
Makes mighty men howl...
And look ! A sad Penguin. Please pass me a towel.

Here come the Adverts
From magical lands
Where crackers go POP as the Snowmen hold hands;
Where everyone smiles
And where life is a dream...
Then I check today's date ! Then I whimper
And
SCREAM.

****

IT'S THE LIMIT.
****

"Let's set a limit,"
That's what we said.
"Five pounds perhaps ?
Per gift ? And per head ?"

We all agreed. It all made sense.
Increase the fun. Reduce expense.
So off I went to buy the treats:
The snowman soaps; the tubes of sweets;
The festive bags of smelly stuff,
Small of course - but quite enough.

And then I looked at what I'd bought -
It all seemed rather mean, I thought...
So maybe I should add a few
Tiny little extras too.
So off I rushed to try again -
A velvet scarf; a silver chain;
A perfume with a fancy name;
A glossy book; a cool, new game.

This time, the gifts seemed more the thing.
I bought some rather super string;
And gorgeous paper; golden bows;
Plus flashy labels (loads of those).

On Christmas Day, at present time,
I felt as if I'd planned a crime !
I knew I'd played an awful trick...
In fact, I felt ashamed. And sick.
I spied the parcels meant for me -
I opened them. Reluctantly.

A jumper made of mohair ? Then -
A shockingly exclusive pen ?
The latest gadget, sleek and slim ?
A vase with gold around the brim ?
A box of chocs (the largest size) ?
Each present was a HUGE surprise.

I raised my eyes,
We all looked heated...
Every one of us had
CHEATED !

****

A CRAFTY CHRISTMAS.
****

I've avoided High Street Nightmares -
I chose all your gifts from Craft Fairs.

A jumper that's hand knitted
From organic, woven straw;
A picture by an artist
Who has taught himself to draw;
A pot-pourri that's just enough
To make a grown-man faint;
A vase that's decorated with
A special, lumpy paint.

A box, brand-new and varnished,
Then distressed - so it looks old;
A rather clever neck-scarf
That's impossible to fold;
A puppet for the children
That will scare them into fits;
A puzzle on a rice-grain
That will make you lose your wits.
Each item is original - a really BIG surprise -
Can't wait to hear your grateful gasps...
And see your tearful eyes.

But here the Craft Fair nonsense stops -
I want some proper gifts from
SHOPS.

****

CUTTING THE COST.

****

Shop-bought presents can be dear -
So be like me. Save cash this year
By giving things designed by YOU
(And all of them recycled too).

I've decorated flower-pots
With jolly lines and cheerful spots.
(The paints were mostly green and red
From ancient tins found in the shed).
I've bored large holes in house-hold bricks
And now they're Christmas Candle-Sticks.

The stones (brought home from holiday)
Are glitter-glued to give away
As paper-weights ! They're rather smart.
While unripe fruits (too small, too tart)
I've boiled and bunged in coffee-jars
With labels trimmed to look like stars.
So
All my gifts were made by me,
And every single one was FREE.
The only snag that I can see...
IS
All that packing took me days,
Until my eyes began to glaze;
The parcels piled against the wall,
I staggered off to post them all.
They weighed me down,
They gave me cramps -

And cost a hundred pounds in STAMPS.

****

DEAR SANTA.
****

Dear Santa,
The world's in a terrible state,
Pollution and poverty, hunger and hate.
The icebergs are melting;
The rain-forests burn;
There seems to be sorrow
Wherever we turn.

The creatures are dying,
The tigers, the bears,
While everyone worries
But nobody cares...
Or at least - not enough to cry:
"Stop !" and "No more !
What's all this grabbing
And greediness for ?"

So here is my wish-list
For Christmas this year -
Bring one Magic Day
Without fury or fear.
One Magic Day when
There's no need to fight;
A day when our leaders
Put everything right.

And maybe - just maybe
The habit will grow...
We'll stop being selfish and angry
And so -

9

Forgiveness and friendship
And joy will increase -
And the New Year will start with
An outbreak of
PEACE.

****

THE NEEDY-GREEDY GROTTO RAP.

****

Santa Claus sighed a weary sigh -
As the letters came
And he wondered why...

The children today want flashy toys,
With a big, wide screen
And a crash-bash noise...
And a brand new app which will drive them mad -
Was it need ? Or greed ?
Were they spoiled ? Or sad ?
Then he heard the News on his radio,
And he lost his smile
And his HO HO HO...

As he heard of floods and he heard of drought,
And the hungry souls
Who were calling out
For a bowl of rice or a crust of bread -
But before he slumped
On his scarlet bed
With a flannel wrapped round his poor old head...
"There is Good News too,"
The Announcer said...

"All round the World, our children spent days
Raising more cash
In a thousand ways;
And at Christmas time, as we knew they would,
They've proved they can
Be kind. And good."

11

So the Old Saint smiled as an Old Saint should -
Then he grabbed his sack
And his fluffy hood...

As he cried: "Our kids haven't changed. Not one !"
And he sailed away
To deliver
FUN.

****

POCKET POEM.

****

Dear Santa -
There's one gift I long for,
(Though the Fashion-World's certain to block-it).
How I envy those cool Kangaroos
When they bounce round the bush like a rocket...

They don't need a buggy or basket
Or trolley (plus coins to unlock-it)
Since Nature provides a neat answer -
A bag, super-stretchy ! Don't knock-it.

I've trudged round the High Street for ages
To pounce on a pouch - if they stock-it !
But storage in skirts and in dresses
Is banned ! Not a hope. And that frock...it
Would sag if I stuffed it with wallets
Or tissues ! The Shop-Girls would mock it.

SO

I don't want more satchels and handbags...
I just want one Giant-Sized
POCKET !!

****

13

SURPRISE, SURPRISE !
****

The shopping's done. I've packed the lot.
I've labelled everything I've got.
I've posted some and boxed the others -
Gifts for parents, aunties, brothers...
I'm just about to slump and smile- and put my feet
up for a while.
I'm just about to take ONE sip
Of tea - but as it burns my lip,
The doorbell rings. Surprise, surprise -
a sort-of friend confronts my eyes.

A sort-of friend I haven't seen since
Boudicca became a Queen.
A sort-of friend who'd slipped my mind,
And here she is ! How sweet, how kind,
In all the rush to think of me ! I weakly offer
luke-warm tea,
As panic strikes my heart, my head -
She's brought a present - wrapped and red.
"Don't open it till Christmas Day," she tells me as
I charge away.

I search through all my precious loot,
for something that will vaguely suit...
I grab a gorgeous paper-knife
I bought for Dad. But hey ! That's life.
It cost a bomb, but I don't care - I'll seem
PREPARED. I swiftly tear
The label off, then fix with glue
A message saying: 'Just For You.'

I stumble back with hair on end -
with inky fingers I extend
My present to my sort-of friend.

****

As soon as she is out of sight - I grab my parcel,
grip it tight.
I cast the paper on the rug
Behold ! A cheap and nasty mug.
The sort I'd never, ever choose - I couldn't force
myself to use.
I wouldn't give a penny for...
I think it's at this point -
I SWORE !

****

SLIPPER SOLUTIONS.

****

This year - I'm giving SLIPPERS
To the people on my list -
So no one will be envious
And no one will be missed.

Our Gran would like two happy dogs - All stitched
with velvet browns;
She'll feel all soft and cosy - Despite life's ups and
downs.
Our Grandad's rather grouchy - So he grumbles and
he frowns -
That's why I've gone and given him - A brace of
Jolly Clowns.

Our Aunt and Uncle love to watch
Those glitzy 'Strictly Pairs' -
They'll soon display their sequins when
They're skipping down the stairs.

The Girls are fond of 'Frozen'- So their toes will
shine like snow -
They'll say: "We'll never take them off !" - And we'll
say: "Let them go !"
The Boys just want to charge about - I'll give them
Hot-Rod Cars...
With lights and honks and screeches when - They
shout: "We're Turbo-Stars !"

Our Cousin's keen on Doctor Who -
He'll strut around with pride...
Each Tardis is a triumph since
They're both SO BIG inside.

For Mum and Dad I've done my best - To get their
presents right -
I've bought self-heating bootees so - They'll stay all
warm, all night.

But as for me - I haven't had
One single pair of slippers !
Who cares ? The rain is pouring down -
That's why I've asked for
FLIPPERS.

****

(Never mind Covid - Colds and Flu' are still waiting
in the wings...)

A FESTIVE FOLK-SONG.

****

A Traditional Crowthorne Winter Lament.
To be sung (with a finger in your ear) to the tune of:
'Twa Corbies.'
Also known as: 'Two Crows.'

****

As I was a-walking through the town
I met a man who wore a frown...
I said, "Whatever's up with you-oh ?
Don't breathe on me if you've got the Flu-oo-Oh,"
(Audience joins in:)
"Don't breathe on me if you've got the Flu-Oh."

He said: "I've wandered round the shop,
Until my eyeballs both went POP !
I need to find, before I freeze-oh,
Something for someone hard to Plea-ease-Oh."
(Audience joins in:)
"Something for someone hard to Please-Oh !"

"It's for my wife I have to find,
A Christmas gift to blow her mind...
I don't know what I'm meant to do-oh !
I'm up a creek without a clue-oo-oh..."
(Audience joins in...)
"I'm up a creek without a clue-oh !"

18

"Should I buy boots I can't afford ?
A useful broom ? Or ironing board ?
Or what about a woolly vest-oh ?"
"Oh No !" I shouted. "Cash is Be-est-oh !"
(Audience, especially the women...)

"OH NO !" I SHOUTED -
"CASH IS BEST-OH !"

****

CREEP AND FIST AND WEEVIL.

****

(To be sung to the tune of: 'Good King Wenceslas')

If you dare to venture out
On the Feast of Stephen;
If you snap your leg upon - Paving slabs uneven;
If you fuse the Christmas lights
Feel a total foo-ool;
If a Fairy stuffed with spikes -
Wrecks your children's Yu-u-ule.

If you stumble in the shops
Tumble down a lift-shaft;
Burn yourself on candle wax - Need a festive
skin-graft;
If you swallow lucky charms
Hidden in your dinner,
Stab yourself on holly leaves - You could be a
WI-IN-NER !

Call a lawyer. Here's our card -
'Creep and Fist and Weevil'.
Christmas mishaps put to rights -
We will sue the evil !
We will bankrupt those who leave
Public pathways icy...
We will take your case to court -
Though our Fees are pri-i-cy.

Contact us by e-mail or
Dial our number quickly;
Press a zero then a star - We will answer slickly !
State your problem, make it fast,

(Time my friend is money)
Though your outlook's sad and bleak -
Ours is always su-u-ny.

If you win or if you lose,
We'll be bright and merry -
How we love the slush and snow - Jolly poisoned
berry !
Choking hazard, faulty wires
Accidents and dressings...
We will count our bags of cash - You can count your
BLE-ESS-INGS.

****

LATISHA AND NATASHA.

****

(Who should sound rather sneezy.)

Latisha and Natasha,
They are people I adore -
But Na-TASHA'S grabbing tissues
And La-TISHA'S nose is sore.

And when they come together
They can rattle any door...
They can BLAST me through the ceiling,
They can fling me to the floor.
Oh !
La-TISH-a and Na-TASH-a
PLEASE
Have mercy. Sneeze no more...

That's when they glare and growl at me,
(As nostrils drip and pour)
"YOU gave this rotten bug to US !"
And that is when they
SWORE.

****

MORAL:

Revenge is sweet
However old -
But better still
When it's a COLD.

(Exit sneezing...)

****

COLD COMFORT.
****

An Advert From: 'HOT HANKY DOT COM...'
(Terms and Conditions Apply.)

If your nose seems to drip like a Snowman's,
If your nostrils are starting to freeze,
Throw those tissues away -
Try 'Hot Hanky' today,
'Hot Hanky' will soothe as you sneeze.

The Reindeer are keen to commend it,
Whether noses are scarlet or blue.
So don't wait for a cold -
Or our stocks will be sold...
Let 'Hot Hanky' warm winter for YOU !

You just need to send us your Password,
Your data, your Nose-Size, your name;
Plus a list of your friends,
Who welcome new trends -
'Hot Hanky's' ahead of the game !

Your Hanky will reach you for Christmas,
It's pricey - but easy to use...
Just iron it a LOT
Then apply (scorching hot)
To your hooter (or toes if you choose).

We're sure you'll be thrilled with your purchase,
We know you won't sniff at a snag YET -
But our Contract will last
While your life trudges past...

23

And your Hanky malfunctions when
IT'S - WET !

****

(At this point, the distressed reader blows
his-or-her nose,
mops an out-pouring of regretful tears -
and exits sadly.)
Aaachooo !

****

A CHRISTMAS CATASTROPHE.
****

(For Gwen Dean and her pupils.)

It was Advent again in the classroom,
And time for the usual play -
The costumes were just about finished,
The props would be right on the day...

The actors were almost word-perfect,
And everyone knew what to do;
It seemed that our scene was a winner -
Then along came an outbreak of flu'.

The Partridge was fine (when not sneezing)
Though she had to drag on her own tree;
The Doves croaked their lines between coughing;
The French Hens were two and not three.

The Calling Birds mimed with their feathers,
And only ONE ring could be found;
The Geese said the eggs made them queasy,
And half of the Swans must have drowned ?

The Maids did their milking in relays,
While the Two-legged Cow stole the show !
The Drummers stayed home with sick-headaches;
And the Pipers brought tissues to blow...

The Ladies made quite a nice circle
Considering THREE of them came.
But as for the Five Lords-a-Leaping...
They limped round the stage looking lame.

We won't have this trouble in future -
The Flu' Bug has had its last fling...
Oh - we'll still have our festive production,
But we won't put it on till the SPRING !

****

(The following poem was the first to launch
'Poems & Pies' in 1985.
'The Nativity Play' went on to be published -
and became a Picture Book.)

THE NATIVITY PLAY.

****

Here is an Inn with a Stable
Equipped with some straw and a chair:
Here is an Angel in bed-sheets,
With tinsel to tie back her hair.
Here is a Servant in bath-towels
Who sweeps round the stage with a broom;
Here is a Chorus of voices
All eager to cry out: "NO ROOM !"

Here is a Joseph who stammers
And tries to remember his lines;
Here is a Teacher in anguish,
Who frantically gestures and signs.
Here is 'Away In A Manger' -
A tune MOST recorders can play;
Here is the moment of wonder
As Jesus appears in the hay !

Here is a Mary with freckles
Whose baby is plastic and hard;
Here is a Donkey in trousers,
With ears made from pieces of card.
Here is a Shepherd in curtains,
Who carries a crook made of wire;
Here is a Boy sucking cough-sweets,
Who growls at the back of the choir.

Here is a King bearing bath-salts,
Who points at a Star hung on strings;
Here is a Dove who has stage-fright
And quivers her papery wings.
Here is a Page-Boy in slippers

27

Who stumbles his way up the stairs;
Here is a long line of Angels
Who march round the manger in pairs.

Here is a Camel who fidgets
With plasters stuck over his knee;
Here are some sheep who just giggle -
And think no one out there can see !
Here is a Herod in glasses
Who whispers - so nobody hears;
Here is a Mum with a hanky
To cover her pride and her tears...

Here is our Final Production,
And though it's still held up with pins -
The Parents will love every moment,
For this is where Christmas begins.

(Aaaachoo...!)

I REALLY WOULD LIKE TO BE MARY.

****

I really would like to be Mary -
The very best part in the play.
I could sit by the crib with my baby
Centre stage ! With nothing to say !

I wouldn't mind being an Angel
With wings and a halo that shines.
I could stand at the back looking holy
And memorise everyone's lines.

I wouldn't mind being a Snowflake
With cotton-wool over my hair;
Or a Page-Boy with myrrh on a cushion
And a tea-cosy turban to wear.

I wouldn't mind being a Robin
With a patch of red stuck to my chest;
Or a Camel wrapped up in a blanket
With a bulge in the back of my vest.

I wouldn't mind being Narrator,
Provided the words weren't too long;
Or the person who crashes the Cymbals
When we come to the end of our song.

I wouldn't mind selling the Programmes -
No, any old part would suit me...
So
Can anyone answer my question ?
Why is it
I'm ALWAYS a Tree !

****

AWAY IN A MANGER.
****

This year, someone said that the dolly
Looked horribly plastic and fake -
So we borrowed a genuine baby...
And that was our fatal mistake.

We thought he would lie in the manger
And make the odd gurgle or coo,
Which proved that we must have forgotten
What actual babies can do.

At the start, he just smiled like an angel
So everything seemed to go well -
Till one of the shepherds felt dizzy
And we noticed a sinister smell.

Then Jesus blew bubbles at Mary;
He snatched at the Inn Keeper's nose;
He kicked half his hay round the stable,
And sang little songs to his toes.

He pulled funny faces at Joseph;
He tried to eat Gabriel's wings;
He screamed at his shiny, new presents,
(Which slightly upset the Three Kings).

He played 'Peek-a-Boo' with the camel;
He giggled at Herod's false beard -
Our play (as a play) was a failure...
Yet the audience stood up and cheered.

He may not be ready for Hamlet,
He may have a long way to go -
But the moment he wiggled his halo
Our baby had stolen the show !

****

(For Ben, Eli and Dylan.)

THE CHRISTMAS DOVE.
****

I am the Dove
With my white paper wings -
I flutter and twirl,
While the Angel Band sings.

But first they're too fast,
Then they puff and they blow,
Till I'm not in the place where the Dove's meant to
go.

So I flap round the manger
To reach the right spot,
But I bump into Joseph - who grumbles a lot !

He gives me a shove
(Which is NOT very holy).
I twitter. I wobble. I tumble quite slowly...

And land on the Camel
Who's wobbling too -
I've unstuck her hump - which took AGES to glue.

She's out for revenge,
So she bashes a wing,
And that's when I crash into Herod the King.

He PINGS the elastic
Attached to my beak -
So I let out a SQUAWK, as the Mice sadly squeak:

'The Message of Christmas
Is brought by our Dove...
We wish you a Season
Of PEACE
And of
LOVE."

****

THE PLAY'S THE THING.
****

This year, we've scrapped Nativities
In case we cause offence
To fragile souls who faint with shock
At tin-foil frankincense;
Or Angels flapping paper wings;
Or Henchmen, shy and tense.

We've also censored Santa Claus -
Quite frankly, he's too fat
And far too fast a driver...
Round the world ! In six hours flat !
And all that creeping through the house
At night ? We can't have that.

We won't wear Snowmen costumes now,
Or Penguin suits. Good grief -
Such fanciful and foolish stuff
Is quite beyond belief.
And Fairies with their magic wands,
They've gone - to great relief !

Which leaves us with a Moral Tale
To show what comes of Greed -
The dreadful fate of children who
DEMAND more than they NEED...
Concluding with a morbid song
That's droned at dreary speed.

So much for joy and merriment,
For fir trees bright and tall,
As carols groan and parents moan,
And snowflakes float and fall...
We've found the perfect formula
To please
NO ONE AT ALL.

****

THE CARETAKER'S STORY.

****

The school was sad and silent,
The corridors grew chill,
No draught disturbed the darkness,
The dust lay pale and still...
Then all the classroom spiders
Came climbing from the sill.

They scuttled through the moonbeams,
They scurried through the night,
They spun their threads of silver,
They wove a web so bright
It trapped a winter magic
And it filled the school with light.

Now strands are strung like tinsel
From the window and from wall -
A thousand patterns glimmered
On the ceiling in the hall.
A swirling message shimmers
And it says: "God bless us all."

The school was sad and silent,
I wandered in a daze -
I woke inside a palace
Where a gentle music plays...
While spiders weave their wonders
For the Christmas holidays.

****

2. THE SPIRIT OF CHRISTMAS.

****

SANTA TO THE RESCUE.

****

Old Santa is a kindly soul,
So when his deer retire,
He nips off to the Rescue Home
To see what he can hire.

This year he hit a problem.
The woman shook her head:
"No reindeer, Sir. I'm sorry...
Would a rabbit do instead ?"
Or what about a gerbil ?
Or a rather charming hen ?
(She's not a distance-flier,
But she flutters now and then.)

Santa did his best to hide
The panic in his eyes:
"I need a creature swift enough
To cross the Christmas skies.
I need a pet that's strong enough
To drag a sleigh !" he said...
And at that anxious moment
Something grunted in the shed.

"That's Lulu," groaned the woman.
"She smells a little bit,
And she's rather plump and grubby,
But she's frisky. And she's fit."
So Santa paid the Rescue Fee
(Which wasn't very big)
Then introduced his reindeer
To their Team-Mate - Lulu Pig.

So if you hear, at midnight,
Farmyard noises in the sky;
Or if you catch the pitter-pat
Of trotters trotting by...
Remember, Santa's MAGIC
And at Christmas - PIGS CAN FLY !

****

WINTER WONDERLAND.
****

How the people blogged and twittered,
How they rang the Press and roared -
And said the 'Winter Wonderland'
Was just a wicked fraud.

"It cost us loads of money, then we queued-up in
the cold.
If we'd known we'd all been cheated - not one ticket
would have sold."
"The snow was fake and fluffy. The Reindeer house
was whiffy !
The trees were clearly plastic - and those Elves !
Completely squiffy."

"The Grotto lights were useless. The Gnomes were
old and fat.
They waved their little hammers - but we weren't
impressed by that."
"Rudolph wasn't glowing and he didn't even fly.
The sleigh was small and dented, Well, it made us
want to cry."

"The Penguins, they just waddled. The Polar Bears
just snored.
Quite frankly, all the adults were absolutely bored."
And as for Father Christmas ! Total rubbish.
He was weird -
And anyone could tell he wore a stupid, woolly
beard."

"The toys were sort-of jolly. And the little kids,
it's true -

Seemed really rather happy...BUT...Refund us, or
we'll Sue !"

****

Old Santa scanned the comments with amusement
in his eyes -
Then he went and packed the presents for his
journey through the skies...

"Some grown-ups," he told Rudolph," Can't see
Stardust any more,
Or recognise my Magic - though it sparkles as
before.
But the children, now and always, hear the
sleighbells softly chime -
And they know their Father Christmas
Was the REAL one,
All the time."

****

(Now - it's time for that last minute shopping spree.)

GARDEN CENTRE GRUMBLE.
****

We drove to the Big Garden Centre,
We waited in long, hopeful lines
For fir-trees all lofty and fragrant,
For ivy that twists and entwines -
Or archways of seasonal holly,
But all we could see were the signs...

This way to the tinsel,
This way to the lights,
This way to the Reindeer -
(Warning - Rudolph bites).
This way to the Grotto,
This way to the Sleigh,
This way to Calendars -
A Glorious display !

This way to the Coffee Shop
Cakes and hot Mince-Pies;
This way to Shiny Gifts
That everybody buys.
This way to the Candles,
The merry Snowman Ride.
(He sang a jolly jingle
As all the babies cried).

This way to the Toy-Shop,
This way to the soaps,
This way to the EXIT,
The end of all our hopes...

We drove from the Big Garden Centre
With bagfuls of stuff no one needs -
Plus a headache, a limp and a whimper,
BUT
No flowers. No pot-plants.
No seeds.

****

HOME FROM HOME.
****

Where shall we stay this Christmas ?
What about Aunty May ?
With her hordes of noisy children
And the T.V. on all day !
And the broken toys and the tantrums
Until we rush away...

Where shall we stay this Christmas ?
What about Mo and Joe ?
Who don't do decorations,
Who just say: 'Yes' or 'No'.
Who never, ever seem to smile,
Which makes us ALL feel low...

Where shall we stay this Christmas ?
What about Cousin Bill ?
Who talks about his twinges,
Who swallows down a pill,
Then sneezes on the turkey
Until we all feel ill !

Where shall we stay this Christmas ?
What about Sister Jane ?
Who boils the sprouts all morning,
Who burns the bird AGAIN,
Who cooks a concrete pudding
That gives us all a pain !

WHERE shall we stay this Christmas ?
What about uncle Fred ?
With his nasty tempered parrot,
And that awful blow-up bed !
Perhaps
For once, this Christmas -
LET'S STAY AT HOME INSTEAD.

****

AN OLD - FASHIONED CHRISTMAS.
****

Oh, give us an old-fashioned Christmas
With toys that are made out of wood,
With gadgets that don't need a handbook,
With children both grateful and good.

Oh, give us an old-fashioned Christmas
With jelly and ice cream for tea -
With carols around the piano
With needles that drop from the tree.

Oh, give us an old-fashioned Christmas
With blizzards and genuine snow,
With snowmen and shovels and chilblains
The sort that we knew long ago.

Oh, give us an old-fashioned Christmas
With water-pipes starting to freeze,
With sparks making holes in the carpet,
And aunties who snuffle and sneeze.

Oh, give us an old-fashioned Christmas
With dinners we'll never forget,
With sprouts and with sinkfuls of saucepans,
With tea-towels all tattered and wet.

Oh, give us an old fashioned Christmas
With jokes and a Pantomime Cow;
With crackers to drive us all crazy
With puzzles to furrow the brow.

With board-games that last a whole evening
And end in a family row...
Oh
Give us an old-fashioned Christmas,
With old-fashioned fun -
BUT NOT NOW !

****

(Or this one on the same theme...)

WHAT THE DICKENS ?
****

I wish the Ghost of Christmas Past
Would whisk me back to when
Christmases were warm as toast -
The world was kinder then

The children wanted home-made toys,
Hand-painted, carved with care.
The halls were hung with holly boughs
As church-bells shook the air.

The mothers tinkled merry tunes
On worn piano keys -
The fathers, wrapped in woollen scarves,
Strode home with frosty trees.

Old friends delivered gifts and cards
All signed in proper ink,
While neighbours grouped round roaring fires
To share a Christmas drink.

Of course, there were some MINOR snags -
The dreaded workhouse door,
The filthy streets infested by
The vermin. And the poor.

The misers who, like Mister Scrooge,
Cared only for themselves,
The criminals like bad Bill Sykes
Who robbed the rich man's shelves.

The match-girls and the chimney sweeps,
The debtors locked in gaol;
The law-suits and the dusty courts,
The hungry orphan's wail.

The swirling smogs. The fatal coughs.
The Thames (which smelled unpleasant),
Plus Tiny Tim and...
Oh, good grief !
Let's stick with
CHRISTMAS PRESENT.

****

(If life gets you down - remember those who have
even worse luck...)

PENGUIN POEM.
****

Oh, pity the Penguin
Now Christmas is here -
His day is the same
As the rest of the year.

There isn't a tree
And there's nowhere to go
For parties and crackers -
Just snow. And more snow.
While inside his stocking
There aren't any treats,
Just boring old fishes
And fish-flavoured sweets.

And the stocking itself
Is so terribly small -
There isn't much room
For a book or a ball,
Or a cuddly toy,
Or some nice, cosy slippers,
(Which simply aren't made
For penguin-shaped flippers).

So he sits on an iceberg
With frost on each leg,
And he longs for a cushion
(Instead of an egg).
Then his sad, penguin eye
Drips a sad, penguin tear -

Oh, pity the Penguin
Now Christmas is here.

ALBERT'S CHRISTMAS LIST.

****

(With apologies to Stanley Holloway and
Marriott Edgar.)

It was Advent at last and young Albert
Was excited - and quite rightly so.
He was hoping for presents and parties
And fights with his friends in the snow.

He sat down to type on his lap-top
A letter for dear Santa Claus:
'Please send me a sackload of Lego
And games for computerised wars...
A stick with a horse's head-handle
Is far too old-fashioned for me -
I'd rather have gadgets and gizmos
And a robot to bring me my tea.'

The little lad finished quite nicely
With his name and a kiss and a Lol,
Then added: NO PANTS (which are boring)
NO VESTS (which are worse than a doll).

Now Christmas Eve crept up quite quickly...
His Mother cooked mince pies and pud,
Then tucked Albert up in a jiffy
And told him to TRY to be good.
Well, this was red-rag to the youngster,
He jumped out of bed in a huff -
And filled half the chimney with holly
And mouse-traps and other such stuff.

At midnight, there came a loud jingle,
(That was Dad, coming home from a Do);
While just overhead on the roof-top
A blooming great sleigh landed too !

Old Santa, he picked up some parcels,
Then chuckled - and cheerfully went
To slide down a big, bendy chimney...
But ooh ! What a painful descent !
Well, Santa's obliged to be jolly -
(It's a CLAUS in the contract he signed)
But what with the spikes and the scratches
His mood was a bit undermined.

He tried to be patient and kindly,
He tried not to shout nasty names -
But he came to an instant decision...
He'd confiscate Albert's new games.

He woke up the lad - and by magic
The pair of them shot up the stack;
Then Santa zoomed off with his reindeer
While Albert clung on to the sack.
For the rest of the night the young vandal
Went whizzing and screaming through space...
The snow gave him terrible chilblains
But it DID wipe the soot off his face.

He came home quite late, Christmas morning -
(Which gave his poor parents a rest)
And as for the gifts in his stocking ?
He had NOTHING
But PANTS
And a VEST.

****

52

SLEIGH-FALL.
****

(Written after the 2012 Olympics...and it is well
known that the Queen
had a great sense of humour.)

The Queen gazed in her looking glass
And sighed a wistful sigh:
"One's Jubilee - (three cheers for ME),
So swiftly drifted by.
And though one's people flapped their flags
One simply can't forget
Flotilla Day - those shades of grey,
Those crowds all soaking wet !

Those soggy singers on their barge,
Hands blue and noses red -
The nippy breeze - the need to sneeze...
One's Husband tucked in bed.
Since then, one's waved at school and street
And boring Super-Store...
But miles and miles - of gracious smiles
Have made one's teeth feel sore.

In fact, one's only memory
Of which one's truly fond
Is when one purred - four sultry words...
"Good Evening - Mister Bond !"
Olympic viewers gasped to see
One's coolness and one's calm -
One's dogs at heel - One's nerves of steel,
One's handbag on one's arm

One grabbed one's 'chute and helmet,
One soared, one skimmed, one dared -
Then jumped. Woo-hoo ! (In posh frock too)
While athletes blinked and stared.
Alas - the magic's vanished,
One's left with yet more rain...
So
When one wrote - one's Christmas note,
One WISHED to leap again.

The Queen took off her velvet gloves,
Her cape and crown as well,
Then, in despair - slumped in her chair
To doze as darkness fell...
UNTIL
She heard a jingle
From a fast and floaty sleigh -
And soon it seemed - (like one who dreamed)
To rise...and ride away !

The Driver, dressed in scarlet
Cried: "Let's go !" and with his sack
They sprang, they swirled - they whizzed and
whirled
Straight down a chimney stack.
They hid some sweets, some games , some treats,
Some teddies and some cars...
Then rose up high - to sleigh and sky,
Two jolly Super-Stars.

Next morning, in her looking-glass,
The Queen spied specks of soot.
"One thinks," she said - "One saw a bed
Where Christmas gifts were put !
Perhaps one's mind was playing tricks
To make one THINK one flew -
But sometimes one - deserves some fun...
And sometimes:
DREAMS COME TRUE.

****

This poem is in memory of our wonderful Queen
Elizabeth 2nd..
Not just her kindness, dedication and faithfulness
but her splendid sense of FUN !

****

The following poem was given to
The Princess Royal,
who wanted to recite it for her Mother,
one Christmas Day.

BAD HAIR DAY.
****

One's dyed one's hair for Christmas,
One's dyed it 'Rudolph Red'.
At least, that's what one wanted -
That's what the bottle said.
But maybe one was careless,
Or left the stuff too long,
Or missed a vital warning,
Or else the shade was wrong...

Because one's roots are Purple,
One's ends are 'Barbie Pink',
The streaks of 'Festive Yellow'
Are enough to make one blink.
One's fringe is 'Santa Scarlet'
(Which doesn't seem too bad)
But add 'Satsuma Orange'
And one looks completely mad !

One should have stuck to 'Boring',
One should have stayed with 'Grey'.
One dreads the morning papers
And what 'The Sun' will say .
One's hidden in one's bedroom
Since early Christmas Eve -
But now one's trusty Butler
Is tugging at one's sleeve...

One grabs one's crown and headscarf,
And hopes one looks O.K...
It's time to read one's message
On T.V. for Christmas Day.

****

(I hope it made her smile.)

****

THE YEAR FATHER CHRISTMAS WAS ILL.
****

"Oh no!" muttered Santa. "What can I do ?
I'm feeling so dreadful, I must have the flu'..".

"But who can I send on the Christmas Eve round ?
It has to be someone who won't make a sound.
Someone who's jolly and rosy and fat -
Now, who do I know who's a little like that ?"

"It can't be young Rudolph - his nose is too bright.
It can't be a Gnome, since he'll hammer all night.
It can't be a Snowman - he's likely to melt.
The Penguin hates flying - and won't fit my belt."

"A terrible problem," agreed Santa's Wife,
(Who secretly jumped at the chance of her life).
She pulled on his jacket, his boots and his beard
And looked so impressive - Old Santa Claus
cheered.

"Just look out for aircraft and comets and such...
And hot air-balloons. And don't swerve too much."
But all Santa's warnings were lost in mid-air -
The first Mother Christmas was no longer there !

****

Next morning, the Reindeer (with antlers all bent)
Touched down with the sleigh -
no one mentioned the dent.
While Deputy Santa wiped soot from her brow
And, dropping the reins, made a big, modest bow.
SO

If your new War-Games smell fragrant and sweet,;
Or your stocking's been ironed, or your room seems
too neat;
Or someone has hoovered the house over-night,
Or the sink in the kitchen is shiny and white...

Or you hear a soft laugh on the wide,
Christmas sky -
Just yell: "You're a Star !"
As you wave her good bye.

****

RECALCULATE.
****

Old Santa's got a Sat-Nav now -
It's smart, it's neat, it's sticky.
He's fixed it to his dashboard - So the sleigh-ride
won't be tricky.
The problem is - the bearded chap
Is quite a dinosaur,
And once or twice this Christmas Eve - the reindeer
think he swore !

"This blooming gadget ," Santa groans,
"It's clever and it's quick -
But all these blooming twists and turns - have made
my reindeer sick.
We've found a thousand alley-ways
Where sleighs aren't meant to stop -
And what with all the ups and downs - our ears
keep going pop !"

'We've whirled round blooming roundabouts
Until our brains have spun -
But have we filled a stocking - or a pillow case?
NOT ONE !
The blooming time is flying by
So Rudolph's in a state -
Yet still the Sat-Nav woman screams:
'TURN RIGHT ! RECALCULATE !' "

"Her blooming voice is spiteful,
And her nagging's a disgrace,
I've never felt so frazzled - as we swerve and spin
and race
And now we're blooming BACK again

In Slough, or some such place !"
With that, Old Santa grabs the thing - and hurls it
into Space !
SO
Your Christmas gifts WILL reach you
In the usual, Magic way...
But if you've asked for Sat-Navs -
Well...
They're blooming LOST.
Hooray !

****

THE SPIRIT OF CHRISTMAS.
****

Midnight.
And your house holds its breath.
It is waiting,
Windows bright with reflected stars,
For the beat of fleecy wings
And a song as rich as Cinnamon.

Sometimes, the Spirit of Christmas will dart
Arrow-swift and angry
Past all the grand and gorgeous doors
Where the welcomes are cold.
Where no glint of kindness is ever found
Amongst the silky, silver ribbons.

Sometimes, she will dodge a swarm of buzzing
desires
To chase the mothy wish
Of a shy dreamer -
Until her shadow leans down
To place a small spark of Joy,
Wild as a firefly
Against the dark pillow.

More often, she will follow the path of the Moon
To a friendly door.
Now, she will listen...
Nod
And swoop to the top of a surprised tree
To perform her glittering miracles.
Warmth will flow from her fingertips
As she loops and lands
Soundlessly.

Then, she will smile at the line of hopeful stockings
And leave her own, most precious gift
For everyone to share.

You cannot catch her or trap her
However hard you try;
Nor stroke her scarlet feathers.
But this year, when every house is longing for love,
Perhaps your door will call to her -
And when it flies open
The Spirit of Christmas
Will weave her wonders
Just for you.

****

THE CHRISTMAS EVE HEROES.

****

(For: The R.N.L.I.)

While you and I were fast asleep - a man was
woken by a bleep...
He gave a groan, surprised the cat,
Pulled on his socks, his woolly hat,
Then raced across the cobbled square - to reach
the glowing harbour where...
His comrades yawned and hauled on ropes,
To launch their boat with haste. And hopes.

The night was bitter, waves were high - our man
spied flares that ripped the sky;
He watched the foam that crashed and growled,
As Winter's cruel demon howled...
He closed his eyes in sudden dread - to shake the
horrors in his head.
"Let lives be saved. Let no one fear,
This night, the kindest of the year."

A shredded sail lurched closer now - he dared
himself to reach (somehow)
The splintered deck, where voices wailed -
He flung a line. At first he failed...
Then tried again. This time it held. - "My crew will
keep you safe !" he yelled.
And as the mother caught her breath,
He snatched her son from certain death.

****

64

When Father Christmas steered his sleigh -
to hurry home at break of day -
Another weary Hero said:
"I think I'll stagger back to bed."
His dreams went whirling, fierce and free - he
crossed once more the angry sea.
He braved the rocks, the breakers wild,
To grasp again a stranger's child.
SO
This year, when the church-bells chime
To tell the World it's Christmas time,
Let's thank those teams who grab their suits -
Our Super-Stars
In Yellow Boots.

****

(Especially for the R.N.L.I. Crew at Ilfracombe
Harbour.)

THE BAKER STREET BURGLAR.

****

(Or: 'Holmes Sweet Holmes.)

One Christmas, our famous detective
Felt restless at Two-Two-One B...
So he balanced his chin
On an old violin
And played a few carols off-key.

His friend, Doctor Watson, cried: "Sherlock !"
As glasses and wine bottles broke...
They decided to sit -
So a pipe was soon lit,
And the room softly billowed with smoke.

With a wheeze and a cough, Mrs. Hudson
Burst in with a nice cup of tea...
Plus a cake on a plate -
Which the friends quickly ate,
(It was quite ALIMENTARY you see).

"Mr. Holmes," wailed the House-keeper weakly,
"A crime has occurred in the night -
My mince-pies were nibbled -
My sherry was dribbled
And a carrot received a big bite !"

"What's more - there is soot on the hearth-rug.
There are hoof-marks all over the slates...
And as for the stocking
I washed - it looks shocking !
It's bulging and smelling of dates."

Holmes murmured: "It's not Moriarty -
He recently had a bad fall...
And leaving those prints -
(Which are give-away hints)
Well, that isn't his habit at all !"

He peered through his spy-glass for ages,
He studied the dents in the snow;
He spotted a thread -
That was woolly and red,
Plus a hair (white and fluffy) and so...

He summoned the Baker Street Urchins,
He offered a Christmas Day Prize,
If they could entrap -
An over-weight chap
With a beard and a scarlet surprise.

But of course, the arch-villain had vanished.
SUPPLEMENTARY clues were not found -
Not a cracker nor sweet -
Not a walnut to eat,
Not one single toy on the ground.

Now Sherlock grew frazzled and frosty.
He stamped on his deer-stalker hat.
"This puzzle needs solving -
My brain is revolving,
Round rooftop and robin and mat."

So Holmes, with the kind Mrs. Hudson
Went searching for seasonal clues -
While Watson spied holly
And gifts bright and jolly
All stuffed inside Sherlock's old shoes !

"Here's a book about YOU !" cried the Doctor.
"And look ! There's a present for me...
A pen and some ink
To write stories, I think -
And I know who my Hero will be."

So everything ended in laughter,
The verdict was quite COMPLIMENTARY...
The Baker Street Cad
Was more Saintly than Bad -
And (you've guessed it) his name's
ELEMENTARY.

****

(Ho ! Ho ! Ho !)

THE CHRISTMAS MYSTERY AT
MONEYBAGS HALL.

****

On Christmas Day morning, as snow flurries fall
And gather in heaps on the garden and wall,
A great cry of horror wakes Moneybags Hall.

"Oh, woe and disaster ! While everyone slept,
A Christmas Eve criminal quietly crept
Past passage and pantry where presents are kept."
The guests start to scream. They open their doors.
They gaze at the smudges on carpets and floors.
"Send for a Super-Sleuth !" somebody roars.

In moments, a figure appears far below -
A huntsman in scarlet who squints at the snow,
"Fresh hoof-prints," he mutters. "Made not long
ago..."

"And here on the staircase are soot-marks. Just
look !
They show us the path that the sneaky thief took.
But was it the Butler ? Or was it the Cook ?
Or was it the Gardener ? Was it the Groom ?
This trail of black dust visits room after room..."
His face wears a frown of suspicion and gloom.

He sees that the Lord and the Lady are shaken -
He snaps: "What's been damaged ? And what has
been taken ?
Don't tell me the robber's run off with the bacon ?"
The House-keeper weeps and she rubs at her eyes:
"They've stolen some hay (which is quite a surprise)
Some carrots and one of his Lordship's mince pies."

But just as that instant, a child spots a clue -
A 'Thank You' note propped in the
Kitchen Maid's shoe !
It reads: "Merry Christmas -
From Me and my Crew."

The Stranger, at once puts the whole thing together
The time of the crime and the Christmassy weather;
The hay and the footsteps - as light as a feather !
Then he taps out his pipe on her Ladyship's bed:
"I can tell you - your thief wore a hood on his head -
He carried a sack and his jacket was RED !"

"He took a few treats for his reindeer, it's true,
But he stuffed all your stockings with packages too -
So I won't say who-dunnit ! I'll leave that to YOU."
****

(And if you solve THAT - here's a small
Supplementary:
Who was the STRANGER ? (His name's
ELEMENTARY.)

****

THE CHRISTMAS BURGLAR.

****

He strode back from the market,
like a nasty great King-Kong;
His bag was full of bargains,
he had picked up for a song;
His eyes were dark as nightmares -
and he'd not been free for long...
For he was a Man,
Who enjoyed doing wrong.

He was sneaking past a mansion house,
to reach his sordid flat,
When a row of gorgeous windows set
him snarling like a cat -
He thought: "I need some practice.
So I'll have a go at that."
For he was a Man,
With the soul of a rat.

He decided on an attic which was
rather high and steep,
His bag slung round his shoulders,
he felt his spirits leap;
"I'll steal a load of presents while
the fools are fast asleep..."
For he was a Man
Who held privacy cheap.

He clambered up the guttering,
unhindered by the slope;
His greed impelled him onwards,
needing neither hook nor rope.

Then he slithered down a chimney,
unafraid of soot. Or soap...
For he was a Man,
Who was dizzy with hope.

He sprawled amongst the ashes of a cold and
grimy grate;
His torch was at the ready, to illuminate his fate,
And there ! Upon the hearth-rug was a
carrot on a plate...
For he was a Man
Who preferred to dine late.

Beside this meagre welcome was a message brief
and neat:
"Here's a treat for dear old Rudolph - it's freshly
scrubbed and sweet."
But, as he stooped to taste it, he could hear
approaching feet...
For he was a Man
Who was doomed to defeat.

A hiding place was needed, but the room was
bleak and bare;
With a single, broken table and a single,
shabby chair;
While every single curtain had a darn,
a patch, a tear...
For he was a Man
Who was tasting despair.

A voice piped from the doorway: "Dear Santa Claus
- it's YOU !"
(A tiny child in slippers and with trusting
eyes of blue.)

"They said you wouldn't visit - but I knew you'd
come. I KNEW !"
For he was a Man
Far too good to be true.

So, instead of stealing jewels, he opened up his
sack -
He gave the child his sweeties, his hazelnuts to
crack,
His teddy and his train-set. His plastic racing track...
For he was a Man
Who would never look back.

And NOW, if you should meet him,
you would never recognise
The fierce and frowning monster, with the evil,
hooded eyes -
This Christmas Eve, you'll find he wears a different
disguise...
For he is a Man
Who is gentle and wise.

His sack is big and bulgy - but it isn't labelled
'SWAG !'
His sweater's lost his burglar-stripes - it's redder
than a stag...
And his face is kind and jolly, with a fluffy beard to
wag...
For he is a Man
Who has JOY
In the bag.

****

73

IF-MASS.
****
(With apologies to Rudyard Kipling.)

If you can spot a Christmas tree in Summer,
Then stifle groans and curses all day through;
If you can hear a ghastly jingle-jangle
When sleigh-bells stuff your head with Musak too.

If you can make a list of cards and presents
For people who will send you something weird;
Then open up a pack of boring tea-towels...
Or friends who send you smellies - as you feared.

If you're woken early in the morning
And do your best to greet the crumpled mess;
If all the meals are late and rather muddled,
Yet still you hide your panic and distress.

If you can gaze at heaps of crumbs and clutter
And try to look SO joyful all the same;
Or forced to play a Quiz designed by Mensa...
Or else an endless, noisy children's game.

If you can welcome someone's sweetheart kindly:
"She's vegan and allergic to the sprouts."
Then smile as if you truly are delighted...
Although you somehow try to hide your doubts.

If you can do your best to feed the toddlers,
Then scrape the awful mess to please the birds;
If you can softly whimper when an Aunty
Munches all your sweets without a word.

If you can wear a Cracker Crown quite proudly
And wish your dreadful visitors would stay...
You are a Treasure and a Christmas Hero,
And what is more -
You've earned a HUGE:
"Hooray !"

****

BABY'S FIRST CHRISTMAS.
****

There's a cracker in the cat-flap,
There's a fairy in the sink
And someone's torn the tinsel off the wall.
The Christmas cards have scattered
Like a flock of startled birds
To decorate the carpet in the hall.

There is chaos in the kitchen
There is custard mixed with sprouts,
There are smears of pureed carrot on the door.
There's a rather festive pattern
That's a bit like chocolate stars
On the doormat and the cupboards and the floor.

There's a teddy in the trifle,
There's a shoe in Grandad's soup,
There's a rattle where the serving spoon should go,
There's a blob of something nasty
On the cloth we keep for best
And the candle (now it's nibbled) just won't glow.

There's a tortured cry of horror
As an ancient lump of rusk
Is found inside the bowl of cheesy snacks.
There's a less-than-joyful outburst
From an Aunty on the stairs
Who's trodden on a duck that really quacks.

While the cause of all the trouble
Sits entranced beneath the tree,
His baby-mind too full to want for dinner -
With a strip of well-chewed paper
And a dented cardboard box...
He's already voted Christmas Day a winner !

****

(Of course - the baby can be a girl.)

A CHRISTMAS BIRTHDAY.

****

"A Birthday at Christmas -
How lovely !" they cry.
They tell me I'm lucky - But don't ask me why ?

Just one set of presents to wait all the year,
Then fifty-two weeks
Till the next one is here.
And opening parcels
Is no fun to do
When everyone else is receiving them too !

I don't like to moan, but it hardly seems fair
When everyone else
Has new outfits to wear.
And what makes me special
I really can't tell -
When everyone else has a party as well.

I don't want to grizzle - but where is the treat,
When everyone else
Has a HUGE cake to eat ?
And I may sound like Scrooge
But I hate it the most
When everyone else has a sackful of post.

I suppose I should smile -
but I couldn't feel glummer...
Why couldn't my birthday
Be swapped to the Summer ?
So forget all your "Happy
Returns of the Day !"
Just stash all my presents and pack them away

Then hide them upstairs
While the world whizzes by -
And don't get them down till the start of:
JULY !

****

MR. GREYSUIT'S GLOOMY DAY.

****

Mr. Greysuit woke alone,
He checked his Rolex. Checked his phone.
He washed and dressed in frantic haste,
So not one second went to waste.
He shoved the clutter off his mat,
He grabbed his briefcase, left the flat
And raced away to catch his train...
(The wretched thing was late AGAIN !)

He took his usual First Class seat,
He bought a boring snack to eat,
He spent his journey tapping keys -
His laptop warm upon his knees;
So office e-mails could be scanned
And every minute neatly planned.

He reached the tower-block at last,
He swiped his card. The door stuck fast !
What was wrong, for goodness sake ?
Was anybody else awake ?
He shouted for the silly fool
Who swept the entrance - as a rule ?

He peered through windows, blinked around.
No sign of life inside. No sound.
No meetings and no teeming hordes,
No warnings pinned to notice boards.
Greysuit slumped. He groaned and said...
"Perhaps I'm dreaming. Or I'm dead ?"

Just then, as snow-clouds filled the sky,
A happy tramp came lurching by.
He wore a beard and paper crown,
"Cheer up," he croaked. "Don't sit and frown."
He slipped a card in Greysuit's hand -
Then hiccupped back towards the Strand...

While Greysuit read, with cold dismay -
'MAY JOY BE YOURS - THIS CHRISTMAS DAY.'
He kicked his phone so far - it flew !
He kicked his lap-top, broke his shoe,
Then kicked himself - and quite right too.
MORAL:
If you didn't log or list it
I'm afraid - you've gone and missed it.

****

CHRISTMAS COLLECTIVES.

****

A Shiver of Snowflakes;
A Jiggle of Jellies;
A Cascade of Cards,
A Splatter of Wellies.

A Comfort of Carols
We all seem to know;
A Glimmer of Candles -
A Shimmering row.

A Sizzle of Magic -
Up there, on the tiles !
A Rustle of Stockings,
A Shining of Smiles.

An Eruption of Crackers:
A Shower of Fun;
A Giggle of Jokes,
Now the Feast has begun.

A Rumble Of Tummies;
A Boxful of Dates;
A Frazzle of Cooks,
With a Clatter of Plates.

A Dribble of Puddings;
A Perfume of Pies;
A Sparkle of Children,
With Stars in their eyes.

A Cavern of Yawns
As the Night starts to fall -
And
A Blanket of Happiness
Warming us
All.

****

IF ONLY.
****

If only the dog hadn't barked at the Cat,
Who shot up the tree to the Fairy -
If only the baubles (so festive and bright)
Had NOT bounced on poor Aunty Mary...

If only she'd ducked when her cracker went POP
And emptied its prize in her coffee;
If only our Dad hadn't raced through the door
To see what the uproar could NOW be...
If only he'd noticed the small, squeaky toy
Which tripped him and twisted his Bad-Knee;

If only the Baby had NOT tried to bite
The box of liqueurs for our Gran;
If only our Mum hadn't served the mince pies
As the horrible screaming began;
If only she'd NOT dropped her best china dish
Which made such a terrible crash;
If only she hadn't forgotten the cakes
Which had burned to a mountain of ash;

If only the Boys hadn't stamped down the stairs
With a drum and a stick in each hand;
If only the Girls hadn't danced to a tune
So ghastly it should have been banned;
If only the Twins hadn't burst the balloons
With holly - to set poor Grandad groaning;
If only the Neighbours had NOT banged the wall
Which meant Uncle Frank started moaning.

If only the lights hadn't blinked and gone out,
As we blundered around in the rubble;
If only the Cat hadn't pounced on the Dog -
So he BARKED, which began the whole trouble;
If only our Christmas had gone as we'd planned
With everyone bored stiff and snoring...
If only the chaos had NEVER occurred...
Well
It would have been ever-so
BORING !

****

MUST - HAVE !
****

(For Sir Ken Dodd.)

What are the MUST-HAVES, this bright Christmas
Day ?
We MUST-HAVE a lap-top that's slinky and grey.

We MUST-HAVE a spy-cam that fits in a pocket.
We MUST-HAVE a shiny, remote-controlled rocket.
We MUST-HAVE the latest in films and in games.
We MUST-HAVE new outfits with smart
High-Street names.

We MUST-HAVE a robot that's programmed to
fight.
Mum MUST-HAVE a novel to read through the
night.
And Dad MUST-HAVE gadgets.
And Gran MUST-HAVE sweets.
And even the Dog MUST-HAVE small,
doggy treats.

As for the food - well, we MUST-HAVE mince pies.
We MUST-HAVE a pudding (the Ultimate Size).
We MUST-HAVE a turkey, the sprouts and the
stuffing.
We MUST-HAVE it all. And we MUST leave out
nothing.

But what if we CAN'T-HAVE the things on our list ?
Won't we be gloomy when something is missed ?
Or will we be happy when (heavens-above)
We share what we DO-HAVE...
Our Laughter.
And Love !

****

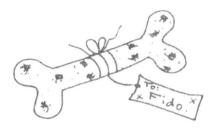

WHO ?
****

WHO
Put the 'H' in Christmas ?
Were they just filling the space ?
An 'H' is no use
Without an excuse -
My frowns have just crumpled my face !

No 'L' never laughed at a Lark...
This 'H' is just causing distress !
But winks hide a smile
With an 'H' for a while -
And LOOK !
How it brings
HAPPINESS.

****

3. MAKING MERRY.

CHRISTMAS IS FOR THE CHILDREN.

****

Christmas is for the children -
That's why we frantically shopped -
That's why we spent all our savings
While our pesky kids
Fretted and flopped.

Christmas is for the children -
That's why we staggered around,
With mountains of mystery parcels
While our pesky kids
Grizzled and frowned

Christmas is for the children -
That's why we jumped-up at dawn,
To dance round the tree with our stockings...
While our pesky kids
Watched with a yawn.

Christmas is for the children -
That's why we sat on the floor
Setting up railways and race-tracks
While our pesky kids
Grumbled some more.

Christmas is for the children -
That's why we munched through the chocs
And tested the games and the gizmos,
While our pesky kids
Played with the box.

That's why we're pulling the crackers
While our pesky kids wait for their tea...
Christmas is for the children

NO MATTER HOW OLD THEY MAY BE !

****

(It's time to open all those Christmas Presents !)

MADE BY HAND.
****

My Granny had knitted a jumper -
It took her a month (if not more)
It was baggy in all the wrong places
And the arms stretched right down to the floor.

The colour was well-worth avoiding,
And the front didn't quite meet the back.
The neck was so tight it was painful
And the whole effect looked like a sack.

She wrapped it with love and with tissue,
Then propped it in front of the tree...
And I knew, without reading the label,
She intended that jumper for me.

I opened it up very slowly
And struggled for something to say -
I knew, if I injured her feelings,
I would ruin my own Christmas Day.

Her eyes watched my face as I fumbled
And of course, I had no choice at all...
"Oh Gran !" I cried. "Thanks ! This is perfect -
The old one was scruffy and small."

I wore the creation to please her
And waited for insults galore -
But instead of the jokes I'd expected,
I came home
With ORDERS for more !

So now, my old Gran makes a fortune
By turning her wool into gold !
And though we all look pretty funny -
Not ONE of us
Ever feels cold.

****

CHRISTMAS AT THE OLD FOLKS' HOME.

****

It was Christmas Day at the old Folks' Home
And the room was bright with holly,
The T.V. set was singing songs -
The T.V. girl seemed jolly...

But Mrs. Green stirred in her sleep;
She sighed a lonely sigh -
And somewhere, in a far off world
She saw her friends drift by:
She saw her first love, tall and strong,
Before he marched to war;
And there, his photo smiling still
Beside an open door.

It was Christmas Day in the Old Folk's Home,
The tinsel snowflakes shone,
The T.V. people waved and laughed,
The morning glittered on...

But Mr. Sadler slumped against
The cushions in his chair -
He dreamed of long-lost Christmas times
When all the kids were there.
The secret places where he hid
The tricycles and toys.
The stockings full of foolish treats,
The laughter and the noise.

It was Christmas Day in the Old Folks' Home,
The tiny fir-tree glowed;
The T.V. stars were playing games,
The cartoon weather snowed.

But Mr. Browning watched the rain
And Mrs. Grey gazed down
At slippered feet that used to dance
So lightly round the town...
And at that wistful moment
The Girl came whirling in -
"Your Christmas dinner's served," she cried,
"So - let the FUN begin."

****

A FRIEND FOR LIFE.
****

(A Poem for Sir Ken Dodd and his Diddy Men.)

One Christmas I woke up to see
A rather odd gift by the tree -
A wonky-eyed Elf which was slumped on a shelf...
Yet still he kept smiling at ME !

He watched while I tried to play SNAP,
His goggly gaze made me flap -
But he seemed sort of glum, so to please Dad and
Mum...
At teatime he sat on my lap !
He grinned at me all through the meal,
And slowly I started to feel
He's been hoping, all day for something to say -
Like someone half-magic, half-real.

On Boxing Day, perched on my bed
I taught him to swivel his head !
He mimed while I talked to myself, then we walked
Down the stairs saying: "Dutter and dread."
And somehow, in less than a week
I'd trained him to sing and to speak !
There was: 'Gottle-a-Geer' and a 'Hacky New Year',
Though his voice, I'll admit, was a squeak.

Quite soon, while he warbled I'd drink
A whole glass of milk ! Then he'd wink...
At poor Aunty Jean - who tried not to scream
When his jokes made her gasp and go pink !
At last, with my miniature man,
We rode to a gig in my van -

He was naughty and daft -
but our audience laughed,
And our travels together began.

SO
The point of this poem is: 'Seize your surprises...
And remember that friends come in ALL shapes
and sizes.'

****

HAPPY RETURNS.

****

I sent a present to my friend -
The sort of gift I'm proud to send.
In fact, if all the truth were known -
A present I would like to own.
The colour and the size were right,
Not too gaudy, not too tight;
In fact, as far as I could see
The whole thing suited perfectly.

She sent me back a tactful note,
She chose with care - the words she wrote...
But I could tell I'd failed the test -
My parcel left her unimpressed.
I think my friend must keep a store
Of: 'Gifts Unwanted' in a drawer,
To be recycled, when in haste,
So nothing ever goes to waste !

At any rate, the months sped past -
Till Christmas-time returned at last...
And in the post - a package came,
Signed and labelled with my name.
No doubt you've guessed what met my eyes -
The contents gave me NO surprise !
Perhaps I should have been upset,
Sent luke-warm words of shy regret...

But since I LOVED the style, the shade.
The tasteful way the thing was made,
I couldn't seem to feel annoyed...
Let's face it - I was over-joyed !

I thanked her in a tone sincere
For quite my nicest gift
ALL YEAR !

****

TIDINGS OF COMFORT AND JOY.
****

The stockings are bulging
With toy after toy -
All packaged and programmed
To seek and destroy.

The virtual warriors
Wired up to fight;
The plastic Godzillas
Whose jaws have REAL bite.

Mega-blast missiles
On Action Men jeeps,
Rotating saw-blades
That give me the creeps...

Transforming beasts with
Their spring-action claws,
Miniature planets
Designed to wage wars...

Night-attack play-sets
And toxic gunge-tanks,
Gift-wrapped and guarded...
For them all - we send thanks.

We're fully equipped
To invade and to kill...
So much for the season
Of Peace
And Goodwill.

****

THE NIGHT AFTER CHRISTMAS.

****

The bedroom shelf
Is crammed with toys -
Most of them built to make a noise.

Toys with levers
And toys with lights...
Computer games for computer fights.

Dinosaurs stomp
Around the mat
Roaring and scaring our poor old cat.

Wind-up puppies
That bark and spin,
Mechanical dolls with teeth that grin !

Gadgets that endlessly
Play a tune,
All of them gleaming beneath the Moon.

*****

But all the same
It's dear old Ted
With his one loose ear
That he'll take to bed.

****

HOORAY FOR USEFUL PRESENTS.

****

Hooray for useful presents !
The stuff I'll use a lot -
(I don't mean boring bath-soap,
Or a pointless flower pot;
Or a silly kitchen kettle
Or a calendar to hang)...
No ! This year I've been lucky -
How my spirit soared and sang.

They've given me a cow-bell;
A parrot who can spit;
A pair of plastic elephants;
A bag of coloured grit;
A chair that seems to wobble;
Some super-smelly cheese;
A rather messy picture
Drawn by happy chimpanzees;
A set of glowing tooth-picks;
A rubber brick to throw;
A large and lumpy parcel
Full of dehydrated snow;
A huge, hand-knitted cabbage;
A box that seems to buzz,
And a thing with loads of buttons,
(I don't know what it does).

Such kind and thoughtful presents
Have been stacked beneath our tree -
And ALL of them are useful...
(Except, alas, for ME) !

****

JUST WHAT WE WANTED.

****

Beware of those beautiful parcels -
Beware of that Christmas surprise;
Shimmery ribbons and tissue,
Are often a crafty disguise.
We unwrap the paper and shudder
At something that somebody bought;
With love and with kindly intentions
And some sort of last-minute thought.

We stare at a terrible T-Shirt;
A book that I'd rather not read;
Another impossible puzzle;
A gadget we simply don't need;
A picture that makes us feel seasick;
A game that we don't want to play;
An object so weird and alarming,
We choke back our horror and say...

"Thank you SO much. That's amazing.
Good heavens. How useful ! What fun.
We've never seen anything like it
And such a bright colour ! Well done."
We squirm and we sweat and we stammer:
"It's JUST what I wanted as well.
You must be incredibly clever -
Whatever inspired you. Do tell !"

We try very hard to sound grateful.
We add, in our merriest way:
"You shouldn't have. REALLY. You shouldn't."
(And sometimes, We MEAN what we say.)

****

A CHRISTMAS CONFESSION.
****

Dear Santa,

I've something to tell you -
It's something you don't want to hear -
You've clearly conceived the impression
I've behaved really well, all the year

But sadly, since first thing this morning,
When stockings and parcels appeared,
I've told dreadful lies. I've been shameless -
If you'd known, you'd have shredded your beard.

I've opened each gift, looking eager.
I've cried: "That's amazing ! How kind !
How terribly thoughtful. How splendid !"
I'm a fake with a fraudulent mind.

I should have been brutally honest.
I should have found courage to say:
"Good grief. This is perfectly ghastly."
But I didn't. I hid my dismay...

And I don't deserve ONE of my presents...
So Santa -
PLEASE TAKE THEM AWAY !

****

IT'S THE THOUGHT THAT COUNTS.
****

(SHE)
I really don't mind what I'm given -
After all, it's the thought that's the thing...
Though I wouldn't say no to a sports-car,
Or a fabulous, diamond ring.
I'd love a luxurious nightgown;
Or a dress, more exotic than smart;
I'd adore a whole ounce of real perfume,
Or a brooch in the shape of a heart.
I could do with more soap and more bathsalts;
And some talcum called 'Passionate Nights',
I'd even be thankful for tissues....
Well, wouldn't you know it ?
It's Tights.
****

(HE)
I really don't mind what I'm given,
After all, it's the thought that's the thing...
Though I wouldn't say no to a Space-Flight,
Or a jet-plane designed for a King.
I'd love an infallible mower;
Or a rather exclusive silk tie -
I'd glide down the stairs looking regal,
With a fancy new gadget to try.
I could do with more aftershave lotion;
And a soap-on-a-rope in a box;
I'd even be grateful for tissues...
Well, wouldn't you know it ?
It's Socks.
****

(BOTH TOGETHER)

Thanks very much for the present,
Thanks very much indeed -
I really don't know how you do it -
It's exactly what I need.

****

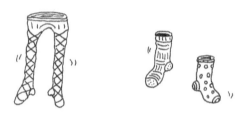

(Leave the stage sadly)

THE CHRISTMAS GIFTS.
****

Oh,
The parcels look magical under the tree,
A stack for the children. For you and for me.
We rip off the wrappers. We snip at the string,
To see what the wonder of Christmas will bring.

But somehow, the gifts we selected with care -
The toys and the gadgets; the sweaters to wear,
Can never quite match all our hopes and our
dreams.
Have we wasted our savings ? It suddenly seems...

That something is missing, or something went
wrong.
And there, on T.V. they are singing a song
Of sorrow and sickness. Of hunger and pain.
So let's travel backwards. Start all over again.

This time the presents we choose and we post,
Will go to the people who need them the most.
To the frail - we'll send kindness, plus someone to
care.
To the lonely - a friendship to keep and to share.

To the outcast - a welcome. To the homeless -
a key.
To the sleepless - a dream of the sound of the sea.
To the fearful - the courage to face a new year.
To the sorrowful - comfort, warm and sincere.

To the stranger - a smile. To the serious - laughter.
With love for them all, in a bright Ever-After.

Then, for ourselves, both in sunshine and stress,
The greatest of gifts
And it's called
Happiness.

****

IF EVERY DAY COULD BE CHRISTMAS.

****

If every day could be Christmas,
If every day could be jolly,
With cotton-wool snow round our windows,
And tinsel and reindeer and holly.
Would we be counting our blessings ?
Or would we be cursing our folly !

If everyday we were woken,
By children an hour before dawn;
If stockings were endlessly emptied;
If wrappers were frantically torn...
Would we be pleased and excited ?
Or would we just grumble and yawn.

If every day there were Grottoes
And last minute presents to buy;
If carols were constantly playing
And fairy-lights dazzled the eye;
Would we wish joy to our neighbours ?
Or would we throw tantrums and cry !

If every day our relations
Arrived on the train and the bus;
If every day there were parties
With crackers and chaos and fuss;
If every day could be Christmas
Would we be grateful ?

NOT US !

****

109

TEN THINGS YOU CAN DO WITH YOUR UNWANTED PRESENTS.

****

1.

You can dump them all in a cardboard box,
You can weigh them down using concrete blocks.
You can wave good-bye - with a smile SO fond
As you watch them sink in your garden pond.

2.

You can turn your trash into bags of gold
If you don't mind rain, if you don't mind cold -
If you don't mind snow, if you don't mind hail...
You can flog the lot at a Car Boot Sale.

3.

If your gifts are worse than a dose of flu'
A Charity Shop is the place for you -
They'll pounce on your Pants and your
stacks of Soap,
While you'll buy a book titled: 'Heaps Of Hope'.

4.

You can pile your stuff, you can build it higher,
You can heat your street with a Festive Fire.

5.

You can turn the worst into Works of Art -
Win a Turner Prize, if you're really smart.

6.

You can bung the lot in a mighty hole.

7.

You can scale a mountain as your presents roll.

8.

You can dig a grave in your flower-bed,
You can try to cry as a prayer is said.

9.

You can line them up on your garden wall,
You can knock them down, you can watch them fall.

10.

You can give them back, with a spiteful cheer,
To your lovely friends - Round the tree
Next Year.

****

A PERFECT DAY.
****

(A Moral Tale For Super-Mums.)

Mum tries to make everything perfect and right.
She TRIES to make Christmas Day merry and
bright.
SO
She mixes the puddings in early September;
She writes all the lists -and she's sure to remember
To sort out the lights - and the glass decorations;
To send all the cards to - our friends and relations.

To buy all the presents, the crackers, the tree;
The turkey, the trimmings, the treats for our tea;
To make the whole house look exciting and jolly,
With mistletoe sprigs and with bundles of holly.

****

And then, on the Day, well - she just seems to flop !
She wakes up exhausted and ready to drop.
She's ratty and grouchy - she snarls at the kids;
She stamps round the kitchen, she rattles the lids.

She grabs steamy pans -
and she scorches the sprouts;
She stabs the potatoes with venomous shouts;
The meal is in ruins - the bird's under-done...
The crackers won't pop - and there's no time for fun.

She hates all her presents, she sulks in a chair -
By midnight she sinks into morbid despair.
SO
We soothe her with cocoa, a kiss and a card.
She tries to be perfect -
She just tries
TOO HARD

****

WHAT WOULD WE DO WITHOUT CHRISTMAS ?
****

What would we do without Christmas ?
No shepherds, no manger, no hay ?
No angels with wings and a halo ?
Dressed up for the end-of-term Play ?

What would we do without Christmas ?
Where in the World would we be ?
Without any holly or ivy ?
The fairy on top of the tree ?

What would we do without Christmas ?
Old Santa, the Grotto, the queue ?
The Elves and the Gnomes in the Workshop ?
The snow on the roof (stuck with glue).

What would we do without Christmas ?
The lights and the flickering flames ?
The presents, the crackers, the laughter ?
The favourite, family games.

What would we do without Christmas ?
The food that takes ages to bake ?
The cards with their robins and reindeer ?
The snowmen who who smile on the cake ?

What would we do without Christmas ?
The caring, sharing, the fun?
The Panto, the jokes and the carols ?
Our walks in the bright, winter sun.

What would we do without Christmas ?
The season we all love the best ?
We say - the World would be sadder ?
But Mum says:
She'd just have a rest !

****

MAKING MERRY.

****

(Have fun with this one !)

I haven't finished the shopping;
I haven't started the cake;
I haven't remembered the currants
For the pies I promised to bake.

I haven't ordered the turkey;
I haven't bought chestnuts to roast;
I haven't boiled mountains of puddings,
My cards will be missing the post.

I haven't wrapped up the presents;
I haven't hung stars from the tree;
I haven't booked seats for the Panto -
Though they're all relying on me...

I haven't lifted a finger
To make their Christmas Day merry -
In fact - I've not budged from this kitchen -
BUT
I HAVE drunk the last of the sherry !

****

(Try to look slightly sloshed)

PEACE ON EARTH.
****

On Christmas Day
There was an unwritten rule...
No one,
And that meant No One -
Was allowed to grizzle or grouse,
Complain or criticise,
Argue or get angry or lose their temper
About anything,
Anything at all.

So we didn't.

And the funny thing was -
For one wonderful, magical day,
No one put a foot wrong.
No one tripped over the dog,
Or ate with their mouth full,
Or forgot to say 'Please' and 'Thank You' -
Or (when the gift was truly awful) tried hard to smile.

So everything was perfect...
The food, the flavours, the crackers, the corny
jokes.
We played games so silly no one ever felt grumpy,
And we had real conversations without fighting
About anything,
Anything at all.

By Boxing Day, we still wore our grins.
A bit stiff now
And strained at the edges
But we did try.

117

Maybe we tried TOO hard, because it didn't last.
Who put fluff on the butter knife,
Who stole the last coffee-cream ?
Who cheated ? You !
No - You ! Not - Me !
Until - soon we were back to normal,
Quarrelling about anything.
Anything at all.

I suppose, Best Manners are like best clothes.
You really love them - but after a bit
You start to twitch - or fidget and fuss...
Until you become yourself again -
And that's better than anything.
Anything at all.

(But some people are never quite satisfied...)

THE GRUMPY CHRISTMAS RAP.
****

CHORUS: Paper Hat - Cracker Snap -
Pass The Parcel - It's The Christmas Rap !

I don't like Christmas when it addles my brain;
They've stuck cotton wool on the window pane -
We know it won't snow since it's going to rain...
So we'll scream if they mention
'White Christmas' again !
Chorus...

I don't like Christmas now it's turning me grey !
My Aunts and Uncles are coming to stay -
My Cousins are driving me out of my head...
And Grandad's snoring upstairs in my bed.
Chorus....

I don't like Christmas now it's making me cringe -
The family's gone on a three-day binge !
Dad's stuffing turkey, Gran's making merry...
And Mum's in the kitchen with a bottle of sherry.
Chorus...

I don't like Christmas since it's making me mad -
I have to watch telly with my Mum and my Dad...
The programmes are boring and we've seen them
before,
While the jokes were invented in the
First World War !
Chorus...

119

I don't like Christmas, when it's making me spit,
There isn't one present that's going to fit...
The clothes are a colour that nobody wears,
The presents are ghastly and they come in pairs !
Chorus...

We don't like Christmas if it's making us blue,
But it's still bound to happen - whatever you do !
So join in the rap, 'cause you know that it's true -
WE QUITE LIKE CHRISTMAS AND
YOU
LOVE IT TOO !

****

THE GRUMPY OLD REINDEER.

****

The grumpy old Reindeer
Have gathered together,
To gripe about life - And the state of the weather
They're stamping their hoofs
And they're starting to curse...
"Progress is rubbish -
The World just gets worse -
Everything's looking for
Someone to blame;
Everything's dreadful
And NOTHING'S the same."

The Grumpy Old Reindeer
Are picking up speed -
They moan without stopping - To rest or to feed.
"The ice-caps are melting,
The snows disappear - Yet Christmas comes
sooner
And swifter each year !"

"There's far too much tinsel,
And far too much noise -
The girls are too greedy - And so are the boys.
They don't want a yo-yo,
Or cute squeaky frog - Just every damn thing
In their fat catalogue !"

Now antlers are steaming,
With venom and spite,
But the Grumpy Old Reindeer -
Groan all through the night...
"The parents are hopeless,

They haven't a clue -
They all seem to want ghastly gadgets - It's true."

The Grumpy Old Reindeer
Are almost in tears,
"What about studs - In their noses and ears !"
But the Grumpy Old Reindeer,
(Although they seem snappy)
Can't beat a GRUMBLE
For keeping them
HAPPY !

****

4. A FESTIVE FEAST.

CHRISTMAS CRACKERS.

****

Does it matter that the snaps are far too feeble ?
Does it matter that the litter starts to fall ?
Does it matter that there's glitter in the gravy ?
Does it matter that the gifts are cheap and small ?

Does it matter that the hats are simply hopeless ?
That the puzzle-game could make an
Einstein bawl ?
That the jokes are all so old, they're
growing whiskers ?
That the wretched riddles drive us up the wall ?

When everyone is having fun together -
And that's what really matters
After all !

****

A LITTLE CRACKER.
****

She's the Girl who makes the Crackers;
She's the Girl who squirts the glue;
She's the Girl who stuck the sticker -
On the one that's stuck on YOU !
She's the Girl who snipped the snapper,
So it starts to over-hang...
Then it singes all your fingers
While the rest go with a BANG !

She's the Girl who stretched your hat-band
So your crown of paper splits;
She's the Girl who picked your present -
So it broke and fell to bits.
She's the Girl who typed the Mottoes
And the Jokes for Christmas Day,
So they're all as old as Santa -
So you all know what to say...

The Chap who creeps around your house
Is ALWAYS a Mince-Spy;
And the way to start a Jelly Race ?
'GET SET' - the children cry !
The Fairy's bound to suffer
'TINSEL-ITIS' yet again.
The Dog without a Nose- will smell
So AWFUL - you'll complain

The Troll who stuffed his ears became
A 'TRIFLE - DEAF' - Woo-hoo !
The 'Knock-Knock' jokes will all be doomed
To end with 'DOCTOR WHO' !
While Tarzan chooses:'JUNGLE BELLS'

To jangle on his phone;
And when the Cat meets 'SANTA CLAWS'
You'll all be forced to groan !
OH !
She's the Girl who makes the Crackers...
She's the one you like to blame,
But you must admit - without her
Christmas wouldn't be the same !

****

A CHRISTMAS ACROSTIC.

****

Cakes rich with currants now Christmas has come -

Helpings of trifle - home-made by Mum.

Rows of roast chestnuts that suddenly POP !

Icing so scrummy I simply can't stop.

Snowmen meringues wearing marzipan hats.

Titbits of turkey to feed to the cats.

Mince pies to munch and biscuits to bite.

Apples to crunch and treats to delight.

Sweets from our stockings - I'm full up ! Good night.

****

(But if you look DOWN the left side of
this delicious poem -

you should spot

CHRISTMAS !)

******

(Now - who feels hungry ?)

SAUCE FOR THE GOOSE.
****

"I'm fed up with turkey,"
Said Grandad last Spring,
"Let's go for tradition - a goose is the thing.
There's plenty of dripping;
And plenty of meat;
Plus plenty of feathers - a seasonal treat."

So we bought a fine Gander
And fattened him up
With barley and biscuits - and bread from a cup.
He lived in our garden
And slept in our shed -
We called him Goliath - and tickled his head.

He chased off intruders,
He guarded our gate -
And no one dared mention - his terrible fate.
But Christmas drew closer,
As Christmases will...
Goliath grew fatter - while Grandad grew ill.

He no longer wanted,
To bake his best friend -
It gave him goose-pimples - to think of the end.
Well...
We all loved Goliath,
So what could we do ?
We had him for Christmas - and Boxing day too !

He sat at our table
As proud as could be....
And shared Grandad's dinner,
And shared Grandad's tea.

****

THE TURKEY'S FIRST CHRISTMAS.

****

Oh, I am the King of the Turkeys -
I'm moody, magnificent, proud.
You can see I'm the best
When I swell out my chest
Till I really stand out from the crowd.

They tell me that Santa is coming,
With presents to hang on the tree.
He relates each surprise
To your stature and size...
SO
I'm sure there's a BIG one for me.

****

COLD TURKEY.
****

Turkey served a thousand ways,
Turkey braised for endless days.
Turkey roast and thickly sliced.
Turkey minced and turkey diced.

Turkey soup and turkey stew,
Turkey curried - Vindaloo.
Turkey souffle, turkey flan,
Turkey tossed by frying pan.

Turkey salad, turkey hot,
Let's all do
The Turkey Trot !
****

THE TURKEY'S TREAT.
****

Christmas is coming,
Don't make such a fuss -
Of course I bought the Turkey !
(But I left it on the bus.)
****

THE VEGETARIAN'S LAMENT.
****

I've given up turkey and gravy
Though everyone argued and sighed -
I've given up eating the pastry
Now I know it's got suet inside.
I've given up pork chipolatas,
Mince pies are the next on the list -
I've even said NO to the jelly,
A treat that will have to be missed.

But I think I could face all my losses
And settle for carrots and sprouts -
If there wasn't one small disadvantage...
That's feeding my Christmas Day doubts.
It sticks in my throat to admit it
When I know they'll be doing their best,
To make me feel welcomed and honoured -
Their first vegetarian guest.

But WHY must they serve me Nut-Cutlets,
All squelchy and sad on my plate -
Oh, why do I have to eat Cutlets
Are Cutlets my ultimate fate ?
Nut Cutlets arrive for my dinner,
Then turn up again for my tea...
Nut Cutlets for supper and breakfast
With no one to munch them - but ME.

Nut Cutlets line up in the kitchen,
Nut Cutlets disguised with a frill -
Nut Cutlets in foil fill the freezer...
It's enough to make anyone ill.
So spare me from Cutlets this Christmas

And don't let my plea go unheard !
Just give me the dates and satsumas
And let's give Nut Cutlets
The Bird.

****

PENNIES IN THE PUDDING.
****

Gran said we shouldn't do it -
We'd choke to death and die !
"You mark my words," she muttered.
"Don't say I didn't try."
She carried on for ages,
Moan and groan and frown
Which only made Mum certain
She couldn't let us down.

She fetched the bowl, the currants,
The eggs, the rum, the flour...
And mixed a mighty pudding
In less than half an hour.
We gathered round to help her
And make our festive wish -
Then placed our contributions
In Mother's little dish.

A pile of foreign pennies,
A token from a pub,
A double-headed ten-pence...
We gave the thing a rub.
We wiped the coins and dried them,
Then added - every one !
While Father stirred the mixture
So no one missed the fun.

On Christmas Day, we steamed it
And served it up for lunch.
"You mark my words - you'll suffer,"
Said Gran, who had a hunch...
For as we tried to slice it

That Pudding hit the floor !
And though we tried to stop it
It vanished round the door !

"It's all my fault," said Father,
As everybody pounced...
"I thought a cheque was safer
BUT
I'm afraid it's BOUNCED."

****

I'M DREAMING OF A HEALTHY CHRISTMAS.
****

We're having a new sort of Christmas,
Environment-friendly and clean -
No waste and no harmful ingredients...
So even our Santa is green !

We won't burn a Yule Log or candles -
They add to the Greenhouse Effect.
We won't buy those spray cans of snowflakes...
Just think of the ozone they've wrecked.
Cigars are a social disaster,
Not to mention a blow to the heart -
And alcohol's much too addictive
So sherry is out for a start.

We're not having festive cheese-footballs,
With all those 'E' numbers inside -
And as for the turkeys and chickens -...
No wonder they're trying to hide.
The Brussels will have to be cancelled -
Insecticide lurks on each leaf;
Creamed potatoes are too calorific,
Powdered gravy beyond all belief.

The pudding's so rich - we'll reject it;
Mince-pies share a similar fate -
The trifle's a foolish indulgence...
Indigestion served up on a plate !
We won't fill our cups with fresh coffee -
(Since caffeine is terrible stuff)
And who wants to risk salted peanuts,
When we've all eaten more than enough.

Which leaves us with bags of bran-muesli,
(Completely organic of course);
Or maybe a small, festive walnut
From an ethically-viable source.
So we'll sit with a glass of cold water
Just munching a slice of dry bread,
And we'll sadly sing: "Come All Ye Faithful"....

The nip round to YOUR house instead.

****

THE SLIMMER'S LAMENT.
****

I've eaten so much that I'm bursting,
And now I've been given a sweet:
If this carries on any longer
I'll be waving good bye to my feet.

I've eaten my turkey and Brussels,
Potatoes and cranberry sauce,
Some pudding, some pies and some walnuts -
Plus plenty of custard, of course.

I've opened a box of cheese biscuits,
Some dates and some fudge from the tree -
I've sampled the chocolate fingers,
And we're having the trifle for tea.

I really MUST go on a diet,
A promise I solemnly make.
In fact
I'll begin any minute...
As soon as I've finished this
CAKE.

****

AWAY WITH THE FAIRIES.
****

There are Fairies at the bottom of our garden -
They're waving at me now, on Christmas night !
There are Elves in pointy hats,
There are pumpkins pulled by rats,
And a Witch who's painted half the garden white ?

There's a Penguin who is singing: "Bring Me
Sunshine'.
There's a line of Lemmings jumping off the shed.
There are Snowmen strictly dancing,
There's a Polar Bear who's prancing
In a tu-tu that is holly-berry red.

There's a crowd of workshop Gnomes who march
in circles,
There's a Panto Cow who's ruining the lawn -
There's an Ogre drinking beer,
With a team of of flying Deer,
There's a Dragon with a fierce and fiery yawn.

There's a pair of Ugly Sisters throwing snowballs,
There's an Elephant who stumps around with style -
There's a Walrus in the pond,
There's a Wizard with a wand,
There's a Santa Claus who wears a scary smile !

There are nightmares at the bottom of our garden -
So that is why my screams are hard to stifle...
For Fairies are the Fate
Of the Fool who loads his plate
With a double-dose of Granny's Sherry Trifle.

****

A FESTIVE FEAST.
****

She'd planned the supper perfectly,
so NOTHING could go wrong -
She'd chosen every napkin-ring, each bowl,
each blade, each prong.
The rich-as-rubies colour scheme,
the gleaming Dinner Gong !

The festive food was fresh and fine and
sumptuously cooked;
No allergy or special fad was missed or
overlooked -
No wonder the assorted seats were swiftly
claimed and booked.

But visitors cannot be forced to take
Behaviour Tests,
So, though the Penguins looked a treat in
spotless shirts and vests,
The Tigers soon disgraced themselves by
chewing fellow guests.

The Camels started spitting - and the
Dormice rudely snored;
The Bears swiped all the honey,
then pretended to be bored -
The Lions tore the tablecloth and picked their
teeth and roared !

The Elephants destroyed their bench by sitting
down too fast;
The Rhino Crew wore wrinkled suits
(the Peacocks were AGHAST) !

Then two exhausted Tortoises turned
up too late - and last.

Someone burrowed through the
cheese - but nobody confessed;
The Wolf-Pack howled in fury, while the Rabbits
grew distressed -
And the Skunks smelt so disgusting - a Gorilla beat
his chest.

The Parrots squawked too loudly - and their
language ! It was SHOCKING;
The young Hyenas giggled and the Mocking Birds
kept mocking;
A Crocodile went SNAP - and crunched the Kiwi's
Christmas stocking.

The Hedgehogs (feeling spiky) wanted games and
presents first;
The Pythons swallowed ALL the pies and very
nearly burst !
And the Monkeys (being monkeys) - well, their
manners were the worst.

So, when the Beasts went off to bed and snuggled
in the dark,
The room looked like a shipwreck - pulled to pieces
by a Shark !
"And that," laughed Mrs. Noah -
"Was a GOOD night on the Ark."

****

A TRADITIONAL CHRISTMAS RECIPE.

****

Stir it cold and steam it hot
And spike with sprigs of holly -
Mix a Christmas Recipe traditional and jolly...

First, you'll need panic and plenty of worry,
Plus handfuls of happiness picked in a hurry.
Stuff a few stockings till bulgy and lumpy;
Add tangles of ribbons (omit if you're grumpy);
Spice with a boxful of lights (freshly blinking);
Then whisk up some laughter, if spirits are sinking.
Throw in the carol you love best of all
And a sackful of cards from the heap in the hall.
Spread parcels and pine-needles over the floor.
Fold in a fairy. Find crackers to pour
On tables (which need to be laden with dishes)
Now scatter with starlight and secretive wishes -
Don't forget PATIENCE. You'll need quite a lot !
AND
As soon as the mixture is sizzling hot -
Garnish your day with a mountain of food;
Some party-games (neither too tame or too rude);
A cuddly Aunty (who doesn't mind losing);
A Granny and Grandad (both smiling and
snoozing);
A slightly drunk Uncle (who giggles and teases);
A Cousin or two (with some seasonal sneezes);
A Mum and a Dad (who are frazzled but fun);
A swirl of small Children (God bless every one).
Agitate well, with old jokes and daft prizes;
Ice with excitement and festive surprises;
Sprinkle with snowflakes as white as a dove...
And serve it all up with a spoonful of love.

Shake it up and share it round
And grab a scarlet berry:
Mix a Christmas Recipe
That's magical and merry.

****

DAD'S CHRISTMAS DINNER.

****

Oh -
We've tried to forget it - Though none of us will...
The Christmas Day dinner - When Mother fell ill !

She curled up in bed with a terrible wheeze -
"I think I've got flu' and it's gone to my knees."
So Dad, sounding manly, said: "You take a rest,
Plus a couple of pills and some stuff for your chest -
While I cook the sauces, the snacks for our tea;
The bird and the Brussels - how hard can it be ?"

He peered in the fridge and the cupboards as well,
He dug out some herbs with a sinister smell;
He turned on the oven, unburdened by doubts,
Then bunged in the turkey and boiled up the
sprouts...
"And now for the stuffing," he said with a grin,
Though he hadn't a clue how he ought to begin."

So he hauled out a cook-book, he laboured
for ages,
Until his hot fingers turned over TWO pages...
Which must be the reason he made (by mistake)
A blooming great Garlic-and-Chocolate Cake !
Meanwhile, the gravy erupted and sprayed
The kitchen with lava - but was Dad dismayed ?

He cast off his apron (the dog licked it clean)
While Father, quite calmly, filled up a tureen
With muddy potatoes, all speedily loaded
Straight under the grill - till the china exploded.
At this point, the rest of us turned up for lunch,
Though the fumes and the fire-alarms gave us a hunch...

...That maybe the meal might be just a bit late.
The turkey, still shivering, sat on its plate;
The spuds were too hard for a hammer to break
As they floated around in a ghastly green lake;
The cake, though it landed with style and aplomb,
And a small, glowing candle - looked more like a bomb !

While Dad, dripping custard (and lumps) on the mat
Said: "Don't look at me - blame the dog. Or the cat."
Oh, we've tried to forget it - That dinner from Hell,
But Mum says SHE reckons
It went rather well !

****

COMPLIMENTS TO THE CHEF.
****

(For Terry)

I have deftly folded napkins,
Placed the chairs in perfect lines;
I have polished crystal glasses,;
I have chosen vintage wines;
I have roasted, toasted, basted;
I have brewed and stewed and scanned;
I have weighed and prayed and tested -
I have steamed and creamed and planned.

I've served Brussels spiced with nutmeg;
I've served carrots honey-glazed;
I've served pies with fluted edges;
(Pastry lovingly displayed)...
I've served turkey stuffed with chestnuts;
I've served parsnips lightly braised;
I've served minted new potatoes;
I've served sauces (rightly praised).

I've served puddings rich and fragrant,
Laced with brandy all ablaze !
I've served freshly ground black-coffee -
Petit Fours - on silver trays.
I have carried off a triumph;
Every course a sheer delight -
I have beamed with modest pleasure,
As my guests all waved good-night.

I have stacked the plates and dishes,
I have soaked the greasy pans...
I have covered up the mixers,
I have stilled the whirring fans.
And now - the feast is over,
I have saved one treat for ME !

It's a nice, soft-boiled egg-sandwich,
With a nice, fresh pot of tea !

****

GUILT ON THE GINGERBREAD.

****

(Or: A Tea-Time Tragedy.)

For our festive tea, for our Christmas guest
I was keen to please - so I tried my best...

There was runny cheese; there were concrete rolls;
There was ham so thin it was laced with holes;
There were home-made dips that I served with
pride,
Though the chilli sauce left us all cross-eyed !

There was salad (limp). There was pastry (tough).
There were shop-bought treats (though there
weren't enough).
There was trifle (cold) served with custard (hot)...
But the dog found that and he scoffed the lot !

While the Christmas cake, which I made myself
From a classy mix on a Gourmet Shelf -.
Did NOT live up to my hopeful plan -
Since the top caved in and the icing ran.

So the Snowman slipped and he lost his head,
And the Robins rolled in a pool of red...
And the Penguins lurched like the Living Dead,
As I hacked a slice for our guest and said:

"Well ! At least there's Guilt
On the Gingerbread !"

P.S.
In the past - pastry cooks used to decorate gilt (or
gild) their gingerbread shapes with real gold leaf.

148

CHRISTMAS NECESSITIES.

****

At Christmas, there were certain things
We HAD to buy...
No one wondered why
But we had to find them all the same:

Circular boxes of jellied fruits,
That stuck in your teeth -
Or lay on the table for weeks,
Unopened.
Tins of mixed sweets
Which were always full of strawberry creams.

All sorts of nuts
Stuck in their shells -
So we could dig out the nutcrackers...
Which never worked - or crushed our thumbs.

Thin trays of sticky dates
With only ONE fork -
While someone else stole the squashiest fruits
And drooled to drive us mad.

Cheap crackers that wouldn't BANG,
But would drop useless presents in the gravy.
Then everyone could say:
'What a waste of money...'
But laughed at the ancient jokes all the same.

There were the cheesy biscuits that made us
cough;
And bread sauce that was full of lumps;
And sickly liqueurs;

149

And exploding chestnuts;
And candles that dripped;
And icing that dribbled,
And a plague of snowmen on the cake,
AND
Christmas just wouldn't be the same without them...

Would it ?

****

A CONFIDENTIAL CONFESSION.
****

Some people are hooked on collections -
Of comics, or cats, or old cars.
Some are addicted to shopping,
Or gadgets, or cinema stars.
Some waste their lives playing poker;
Or betting on horses; or goals;
Or climbing up tall, snowy mountains,
Or crawling down deep, gloomy holes...

Some passions can give us a purpose.
Some make us mad. Or shambolic.
So I must stand here and confess it...
I am a sad CHOCOHOLIC.
It started quite small with Maltesers:
One or two - or (if pushed) three or four;
But somebody gave me a Freddo,
And then I was craving for more.

The Universe opened before me -
Galaxy ! Milky-Way ! Mars !
And soon I was on to the hard stuff...
Expensive and hand-crafted bars.
I couldn't face birthdays or Christmas
Without my luxurious fix -
Gift-wrapped and glittering goodies...
Heroes or Snickers or Twix.

I tried to deny my affliction,
I told myself Aeros were light.
But soon, I was living for chocolate -
The dark and the milk and the white.
It was Coco-Pops (neat) for my breakfast,

Chocolate drinks late at night...
I was willing to kill for a KitKat
And I knew I was losing the fight.

I am pitiful, weak-willed...and dreaming
Of chocolate Santas to buy.
Excuse me - I'm starting to dribble...
I'm off to the Sweet Shop.
Good bye.

****

(Or at Easter, it's - 'Chocolate Bunnies'.)

THE ELF AND THE SNOWMAN.

****

The Elf and the Snowman
Who stood on the cake
Are back in their tin
With a rattle and shake.

And there they will stay
For a dark, dreary year -
The Elf has a holly leaf
Jammed in one ear.

The Snowman, with icing
Still glued to his base,
Has a small, plastic Penguin
Pecking his face.

Yet the Elf and the Snowman
Still smile and still dream
Of magical tea-times,
Of crackers and cream...

And marzipan lawns
For a sugar-white floor...
And they're counting the days
Till it's Christmas once more.

****

A JOLLY CHRISTMAS CAROL.
****

(To The Tune Of: 'When This Lousy War Is Over...')

When this Christmas Day is over
No more festive food for me...
No more Brussels for my breakfast,
No more stuffing for my tea...

No more cakes or pies or puddings,
No more cream to pour like rain -
I will just eat bread and water
Till
My trousers fit again.

****

THE NORTH WIND DOTH BLOW.
****

The wind, it bloweth fierce and fast,
Our fences tremble in the blast -
The local birds have lost their feathers,
This is the worst of Winter Weathers.

It's shattered windows, battered sheds,
It's blown old ladies from their beds,
It's rattled rooftops, clattered bins...
My neighbours shiver in their skins.

"It's all your fault," they crossly claim.
"You're the vandal. You're to blame !"
They charge at me with angry shouts -
And all because
I ATE MY SPROUTS.

****

(And now a Christmas message from Santa -
who has almost burst his buttons.)

155

SANTA'S SHRINKING SUIT.
****

Mother Christmas couldn't stop -
herself from rudely giggling,
As Santa squeezed inside his suit -
with heaves and huffs and wriggling,
The buttons flew - he wheezed and blew,
His chins were gently jiggling.

'What's happened to my Christmas Kit," -
said Santa turning white...
"My scarlet jacket's far too small -
my belt is far too tight...
My zips won't zip - I dread my trip,
Around the sky tonight."

"Your outfit hasn't changed one bit." -
his jolly Wife explained,
"It hasn't shrunk. It's YOU that's grown -
I know you've stretched and strained....
But midnight treats - and tempting sweets
Plus puddings should be blamed."

'In fact," she added cheerfully -
"Your problem's no surprise !
So don't feel stressed or sorrowful -
before you ride the skies...
The children know - You're kind and so,
They LOVE your shape and size."

Then Mrs. Claus nipped out to find -
Where comfy clothes were kept,
She brought a bigger, better suit...so now
Old Santa leapt

Inside the sleigh - and whizzed away,
To YOUR house while you slept.

But Mrs. Santa smiled and said:
"This happens EVERY year.
He'll race and zoom from room to room -
while magic gifts appear...
Then soon begin - To look SO thin,
And Super-Fit -
He'll
CHEER !

****

5. MORE SANTA - SAGAS.

MOLAR MORAL.

****

Poor Santa had a toothache - after munching
Christmas Pud -
The Dentist (Mr. Snowman)
Froze his molars, which was good.
The Snowman's arms were twiggy
So he kept a bunch of spares
In case he snapped a finger as he carried out repairs.

He prodded round in Santa's mouth - He scraped
the mince-pie stains;
Until, at last he shouted:
"Here's the root of all your pains !"
With pliers and with gusto
He began to tug with skill...
There came a sudden, scary CRACK - and Santa
felt quite ill !

"I've only lost a thumb or two," - the Dentist proudly
cried;
"And here it is ! The holly sprig -
That stuck and spiked inside !"
So Santa paid with buttons
For his Hero's snowy vest,
Then ate a bowl of custard...Sometimes
comfort-food is best !

The Moral Is:

Protect your teeth
From stuff that tends to tarnish...
And if you're given Christmas treats -
Don't EVER eat the Garnish.

****

A BOOTIFUL CHRISTMAS.
****

One winter, when it drizzled for dreary days and
weeks,
Santa found his wellie-boots
Were full of holes and leaks.
"You'll have to buy some new ones," his Wife said
(firm yet kind),
So off they trudged, through sleet and snow
To see what they could find.

Well, all the shoe-shops shimmered with wellies
wild and weird -
But Santa's socks were soggy
So he faced the deed he feared.
He opened up his wallet. He told the girl his size -
Then heard her long and merry list
With panic in his eyes.

"Would Sir like these, with tassels ?
Or yellow ones with flowers ?
Or some with stars and comets,
And lights that blink for hours ?
Or maybe Royal Purple ? (A pair to wear with
pride).
Or else a Doctor Who design
(With lots of room inside) !

Or zebra stripes ? Or leopard spots ?
Or grey, with rhino-wrinkles ?
Or green with froggy, goggle eyes ?
Or these - the cow-bell tinkles !"
Poor Santa felt all flustered.
He stared at reds and blues.

He sighed and groaned and shuddered,
Till a Snowman said: "I'll choose."

That's why, on Christmas morning, when you pull
your curtains back _
(And you happen to be lucky)
You'll spot Santa with his sack...
His hat, his sleigh, his reindeer
And his BOOTS...
You've guessed - they're BLACK !

****

BETTER LATE THAN NEVER.

****

(Many years ago - a note was found up a chimney
at Whitley Bay. It was a letter for Father Christmas,
signed by a boy called Gavin London. He wrote: 'I
wish I had a Indians feather hat, a bow and arrows,
a pair of tites and a tommy hork. I hope you and
your dear old rain-deers are very well...')

Old Santa had slumped on his sofa
To stare at the box before bed -
When the Newsreader turned to the camera:
"And finally, viewers...' she said.
"A note has been found up a chimney
By builders in far Whitley Bay -
It must have been stuffed up the fireplace -
Then lost - or just blown far away."

"The message was written for Christmas
Requesting an Indian Set -
With feathers and arrows and war-paint -
But it hasn't reached Santa Claus yet !"
Poor Santa spilt most of his cocoa,
He sprang from his seat with a frown !
"I'll have to deliver those parcels
I CAN'T let the little lad down."

His Wife, in her red, woolly nightgown,
Said: "Don't get yourself in a state.
I know it's a heartbreaking story -
But what can you do ? You're too late.
What if you packed up a stocking
And managed to find the lost boy ?
By now, he's a grey-haired old Grandad
Who won't want a Tomahawk Toy !"

He knew she was right - but the nightmare
Was something he couldn't accept...
So, as soon he heard a soft snoring,
Away from the Igloo he crept.
He loaded his sack full of presents
Then saddled up Rudolph for flight.
They soared through the sky like a comet
To try to put everything right.

They landed beside a Police-Box
That seemed a familiar Blue -
The door was flung wide at their jingle...
Revealing (of course !) Doctor Who.
In no time, a gadget was crafted
To take them to Christmases Past.
It wasn't a traditional transport -
But at least you could say -
It was FAST !

So Santa adjusted his seatbelt
And sped through the magical air -
To slide down a Whitley Bay chimney -
Then vanished
With seconds to spare !
And somewhere tonight - there's a Grandad
Who dreams of a strange Christmas Day...
When he thought he saw one Robot Reindeer
With a Space-Ship
Instead of a sleigh !

****

CYBER SANTA.
****

This winter, Father Christmas gazed in
gloomy disbelief,
At heavy heaps of letters -
Then he turned a brand new leaf.
Which means he's now on e-mail
And on Face-Book too. Good grief.

He's even joined the Twitter Crowd, which frankly
isn't wise.
He's gone and told the whole wide world
His problem with mince-pies...
His fear of skinny chimneys
AND his scarlet-trouser size !

He says he has a squillion friends (who all want
gifts and toys)
And though this is the kind of thing
A jolly chap enjoys -
The logging and the blogging
And the constant tapping noise...

Can even test the patience of a Saint, or kindly man
(Who, by mistake on e-bay
Went and bought a plumber's van) !
"ENOUGH," cries Santa. "Pull the plug !
I need a fool-proof plan."

"And all because I realise - the biggest Fool
was Me !
We don't need Techno-Christmases,
We need a starry tree,
Plus party games and silly jokes,

And fruity cakes for tea,
To share with all our PROPER friends."

And guess what ?
I agree.

****

SNOW - BOT WARS.
****

(Because I'm a fan of 'Robot Wars'.)

The Robots were having a party,
They nibbled their trays of tin-foil;
They crunched up their screws (ready salted),
They knocked back their buckets of oil...

They danced to a band (Heavy Metal),
They flirted, as Robots will do.
Sir Killalot fancied Matilda,
But Bash rather fancied her too.
They handed out gifts in the moonlight -
Matilda was glinting with joy -
There were rings made from recycled engines
And handbags too tough to destroy !

But Bash had become to feel jealous,
And Killalot rose to the bait -
"Matilda is mine !" he exploded,
But his muse rattled coyly: "Too late !
I've fallen for someone exciting -
He's steamy and terribly strong,
He says I'm his own Christmas Cracker
And he's built like a junkyard King-Kong !"

Then in crashed a HUGE Robot Santa,
His beard had a silvery glow,
His wellingtons clanked past his rivals
And he carried some steel-mistletoe.
Matilda ran off with her Hero
To live at the Magnetic-Pole...
While Killalot ran round in circles,
And Bash threw himself down a hole.

The Robots were having a party,
It ended in chaos and woe...
But deep in his underground Grotto
The Santa-Bot clanged:
"Ho ! Ho ! Ho !"

****

A STRESS-FREE CHRISTMAS.
****

"Christmas," grumbled Santa, "Grows more
stressful every year,
As humps and bumps and cameras
And yellow lines appear !
I can't park on the roof-tops, I can't speed through
the sky -
Without the sound of sirens
As the Flying Squad swoops by !"

"And as for 'Traffic Calming' (which has left my
nerves in shreds)
If the Reindeer go much slower, they'll be snoring in
their sheds !
I could decorate the Grotto
With my summonses and tickets -
The rules and regulations drive me crazy !
Make me sick - It's..."

"Enough to test the patience of a better
Saint than I !
Now they're sticking speeding limits on the
Comets ! Why, oh why ?
So I squeeze between two bollards
And give way to moth and bat -
Could YOU fill all the stockings for the children ?
Tell me that !"

He zipped his scarlet jacket, grabbed his bulgy sack
and boots,
He set the Sleigh to 'Light Speed' and
He didn't give two-hoots !
He yelled: "Remember Concorde !"

As the Reindeer steamed and rumbled;
And down the waiting chimneys - all the Christmas presents tumbled.

His blotched and blurry picture - flashed across a million screens;
While the wardens sat with notepads, noting down the shocking scenes.
But a Sleigh without a number
Is extremely hard to trace !
So they couldn't capture Santa - (though they THOUGHT they knew his face).

"Christmas," panted Santa. "Grows more stressful every year !
But do I let it bother me ?
Or slow me down...
NO FEAR."

****

WINTER WATCH.
****

'The Winter-Watch' Teams have been searching
For somewhere exciting this year -
They want to count cute little Penguins,
Plus Polar Bears, Snowmen and Deer...
And, would you believe it - they're filming !
Though no one's allowed to say where -
They're led by a Gnome from the Workshop
And a Fairy with fluffy blonde hair.

"Oh look !" she cries, full of amazement:
"A Bear ! And it's chasing its food...
What a pity it's one of your Sound-Men."
(The Gnome mumbles something quite rude).
They hurriedly switch to the Snow-Cam...
Could that be a Walrus on Skis ?
But no ! It's a rare flying Reindeer
Who swoops above sparkly trees.

Meanwhile, in a shivery Igloo
The Camera-Man waits through the night,
To capture two quarrelling Snowmen
With snowballs - all ready to fight.
They're vicious, they're nasty, they're cheating -
They've chosen to throw cubes of ice !
So one of them's just lost his carrot
And one's lost his hat. That's not nice.

A Snow-Lady comes to the rescue,
With a bagful of prizes to share -
They both grab a handful of buttons
Plus gloves - as they fly through the air...
The Gnome starts to twitch and to fidget,

He's noticed a bright, scarlet glow -
He speaks in a soft T.V. whisper:
"That's our Rudolph ! With Head-Lamps you know !"

An Elf, at that moment, squawks: "Penguins !
They've waddled in lines from the East,
All dressed in their Head-Waiter costumes
To serve up our Christmas Day feast."
So that is the end of the programme -
So only the Spy-Cam can see
A Sleigh, touching down in the starlight,
As the Fairy nips back to her tea.

****

THE APPRENTICE.

****

One day in December, beside his log fire,
Old Santa Claus mutters: "I have a desire
To find an Apprentice, to train and inspire."

The sign by the Grotto said: 'Interviews Here -
The Applicants need to like chimneys. And Deer.
And very long hours - for just ONE night each year.'

Now, Santa had hoped for The Merry. The Keen.
But the Snowmen looked cold and the Penguin
looked mean;
While the thought of a Sleigh-ride turned both of
them green.

The Fairy could fit both her feet in one boot !
The fat Polar Bear couldn't button his suit;
And Jolly the Gnome was a cross little brute.

The Robin complained that the fluff made him
sneeze;
The Walrus found smoke-stacks a rather tight
squeeze,
And he couldn't sit down - since he didn't have
knees.

By now, poor old Santa felt frazzled and tired -
Not ONE single creature had what he required !
So he sat on an iceberg and growled:
"You're all FIRED !"

But nobody minded - they all said: "You know
Nobody else wears a beard - white as snow.
And nobody else has your loud:
"Ho ! Ho ! Ho !"

"You're our favourite Saint, you're a fabulous flier -
So why would you need an Apprentice to hire ?
The answer is simple...
DON'T EVER RETIRE !"

****

A SENIOR MOMENT.
****

Retirement's a teasing and ticklish thing -
These days, my spectacles dangle from string !
Or else they are left in a puzzling place,
While laughter-lines crumple and crinkle my face.

There's a twinge in my back and a creak in my
knees,
And I can't touch my toes, and I can't find my
keys...
I'm asleep half the day - I'm awake half the night,
(Did I put out the cat ? Did I turn out the light ?)

Now I've wandered downstairs, though I don't know
what for -
It was something IMPORTANT and URGENT, I'm
sure.
So I'll look at my list, since I seem to remember
There's something I simply MUST do in December.

A blizzard is blowing, I'll need a warm coat -
But where am I going ? And where is the note
I wrote to remind me my name and address ?
My mind has gone blank. It's excitement I guess...

But WHY am I smiling ? And what should I do ?
I'll rummage around and I'll hunt for a clue...
A big, scarlet jacket ? Two boots, shiny black ?
A hat with a bobble ? A huge, bulgy sack ?

A whole team of Reindeer ? A Sleigh parked
outdoors ?
Good grief - I've remembered !

I'm Old Santa Claus.

****

NAME THAT SLEIGH !
****

(Spoken by Santa himself...)

This year, I launched a contest - in my cool and
sparky way:
I asked the Winter World to choose - a name
I could display,
In red - or maybe silver ?
On my famous, magic Sleigh.

At once, a foolish Penguin- with a waddle and a
towel,
Suggested 'Sleigh-Mc-Sleigh-Face' - but the Bears
began to growl.
They wanted 'Festive Flyer'
(Which was hooted by an Owl).

The Fairies waved their winter wands - and wished
for 'Shooting Star'-
The Wolf-Cubs fancied 'Sacks-Away' - the
Snowmen flew quite far
To offer: 'Rocket Racer'
While an Elf yelled: 'Christmas Car'.

The Gnomes liked 'Jolly Jingles' - and the Reindeer
shouted: "Please !
We want 'The Rudolph Rover' - or the 'Super-Sonic
Sneeze'..."
Until I groaned and said: "Enough !
My brain's begun to freeze."

I sorted through my mighty list -
beside my fire and fretted,
As Mrs. Santa mopped my brow - with snowballs
while I sweated...
Until at last, I chose the words
That wouldn't be regretted.
BUT
Whatever had I chosen ? And WHO had won the
prize ?
Away I sailed inside my Sleigh - Her name flashed
round the skies !
I'd called her: 'Santa's Space-Ship'
Which had come as no surprise -

That's the one I wrote myself
So
I won ALL the pies.

****

THE SPIDER'S WISH-LIST.
****

The Spider in the bathroom wove a heavy-duty
thread,
From the nozzle of the shower
To the light-bulb overhead;
And all along the webbing, she hung her stockings
out,
Spider-Claus would come tonight,
She knew without a doubt.

In thin and scrawly writing, she wrote eight tiny lists,
Attached with care and cunning,
And with sticky, silver twists.
'A purple fly. A golden bug. A centipede. A flea.
A wasp. A moth. a beetle, and...
A Husband just for me.

She snuggled in the centre of her web so fine and
neat,
And listened in the moonlight
For the sound of spider feet -
And there ! Straight up the plug-hole, a scarlet
spider crawled !
With a silky sack of parcels
Which he tugged and heaved and hauled.

'Dear Santa ! You have found me where I dangle
high above...
You have granted all my wishes,
Step inside, my own True-Love !"
Our Spider sighed with wonder at the lovely gift-
wrapped flies -

178

Then she ATE her brand, new Sweetheart
With contentment in her eyes.

****

(Or if you are squeamish....)

'But the Scarlet Spider vanished in an instant - ran
away,
So our Spider lost her dinner
And her Hero's safe...
Hooray !'

****

IN THE GROTTO.

****

(This should be sung, with immense feeling, to the tune of that splendid Elvis song: 'In The Ghetto'. It has been tried & tested in several garden sheds.)

As the wind moans
On a cold and stormy winter day,
A poor little penguin blows away
From the Grotto !
And Old Santa groans.
'Cause if there's one thing that he can't bear
It's a Penguin whizzing through the air
Round the Grotto.

Children, you must all have heard
A Penguin's not a normal bird -
It is stumpy and its shape far from slim,
It's not designed for flights,
It's too scared of heights,
It prefers the salty sea and chooses to swim.

Well, the wind loops,
And a frightened little bird with a frozen beak
Spins in the sky with a mournful squeak,
Round the Grotto !
And its flippers droop;
So its lonely cries are heard all night
It's a pitiful sound. It's a pitiful sight
From the Grotto.

Then at dawn comes inspiration. Old Santa boards
his sleigh,
He shakes the reins. He gives a cry,
Rudolph rides the snowy sky,
And the Snowmen yell...
As the crowd gathers round to watch the chase,
Penguin and Reindeer in a circular race
Round the Grotto !

But it all ends well - In the Grotto...
And the Penguin's safe - the Snowmen cheer,
The sleigh bells jingle, it's a Brand New Year
In the Grotto.
And Old Santa Smiles !

****

MERRY MAIL.

****

When Santa reaches home once more - his poor
old brain is tired and sore -
He's caked in soot from hood to foot,
Too tired to slam the Grotto door.
He staggers to his comfy chair, he brushes frost
from boots and hair;
He toasts his toes then starts to doze
While Snowmen sky-dive through the air.

He dreams of stockings, stuffed and full - with
games and scarves of stripy wool;
The gifts, the sweets, the super treats,
The crackers that he loves to pull.
He hears a jingle far-away, the creak of wheels ? A
phantom sleigh ?
But when he wakes his old head shakes...
No strangers come on Christmas Day.

He sighs, he stretches, rubs his eyes - The fire still
glows (to his surprise).
Has someone crept while Santa slept,
To bring a plate of hot mince-pies ?
And all around the Christmas Tree are shapes that
glitter - merrily !
He blinks and smiles. "These shiny piles
Of Cards and Gifts...are all for ME ?"

His jolly Wife is full of cheer, they share the fun with
Elves and Deer -
Plus Penguin teams, till starlight gleams
And Santa mops a happy tear.

But WHO could make his hopes come true ? -
It wasn't me. It wasn't you...
But I've heard tell a Silver Bell
Can call the Magic Postal Crew !

They tiptoe round an unlocked door.
They nod to hear a Saintly Snore...
Then softly run, to spread good fun
And Christmas Joy -
It's what they're for.

****

(For our own Jolly-Postmen - or (of course) our
Merry Post-Lady.)

THE POSTMAN PUZZLE.

****

Each year, Old Santa likes to take a little
look-around...
This year, he landed quite near me,
And gasped at what he found.
"Good grief," he groaned. "I can't believe my
ancient, misty eyes !
When I deliver presents through the frosty,
winter skies..."

"I tuck my old, red trousers in my fleecy,
cosy boots -
But I've just seen the Postman
And he doesn't care two hoots
For snow or windy weather - if it's raining,
or its not -
He just pulls on some Summer SHORTS -
He seems to think it's Hot !"

"So even when it's freezing - and his knees are
turning blue -
He makes me feel a Super-Wimp !"
Then off Old Santa flew...
"I need some shorts," he told his Wife.
"Instead of woolly clothes."
(A passing Snowman laughed so much
He almost lost his nose !)

But Mrs. Santa simply smiled and said:
"The children know
You HAVE to wear your famous suit
Each time the Reindeer go

A-whizzing round the big, wide World -
Your picture tells them so !"

"Imagine how the little ones will feel,
when stars are bright,
And you appear with hairy legs -
One crisp December night ?
For goodness sake ! You'll give them all
A really nasty fright !"
SO
Santa WILL arrive this year -
wrapped up all warm and happy,
In proper Winter wellies
And his TROUSERS (red and flappy).
While jolly Mister Postman - in his usual, festive
way
Will wear a pair of scarlet shorts
And wave at Santa's sleigh.

****

(Yes ! Our Post-Lady also wears shorts.)

BETWEEN THE LINES.

****

The Post Office Penguin, delayed by a strike,
Arrived at the Grotto and fell off her bike.
She brandished a letter and cried with a croak:
"I think it's for you, but the writing's a joke !"

Now, the note for Saint Nick was incredibly scrappy,
Enough to make anyone moody and snappy -
The Snowmen were shocked - and the Reindeer
said: "Hay !
That list is an insult. Just throw it away."

But Santa just laughed, counted errors galore -
"I've never been called: 'Dear Old Satan' before !
Perhaps the poor writer was weary. Or worried.
Or slightly distracted. Or harassed. Or hurried...."

"And maybe these blobs could be misunderstood -
But I can't take offence - when intentions are good."
Then he loaded the Sleigh and he sped through the
night,
Hoping the parcels he'd packed were just right...

But what did he leave by the Scribbler's Tree ?
A book about spelling - called: 'I Before E !' ?
Some shiny new pens for a shiny new start ?
Or a colourful, Christmassy-Handwriting-Chart ?

I'm afraid - I can't tell you - but Heavens Above !
What does it matter ?
Those gifts came with
LOVE

****

SANTA'S RAILWAY BLUES.

****

Father Christmas, just for fun - thought he'd join the
Santa-Run !
He'd meet new friends - He'd feel more fit;
He sorted out a well-worn kit...
"I'll line up with the plump, the slim - and NOBODY
will know I'm HIM !"

"I can't arrive with Deer and Sleigh - since that
would give the game away;
So, being quite a careful chap
I'll check the venue on the map."
He scratched his beard, he racked his brain - Then
cried: "I know. I'll go by train."

He set off early, brought his lunch - an athlete
needs a cake to munch.
The mean machines spat out his card,
But Santa found a friendly Guard,
Who said: "There's been a slight delay. Signal
failure - Guildford way."

So Santa snacked as hours flew past - a crowded
train arrived at last:
He squeezed between two grouchy men
Who phoned and moaned till ten-past-ten.
"We're here I think," said Santa. "Good !" The
engine stopped, but no one stood...

A squeaky voice announced: "We're stuck - We'll
clear the line with any luck.
We'll soon get going. Wait and see..."
Poor Santa rubbed his nose. And knee.

He peered outside. He groaned: "Good grief !
We've all been stopped by one wet leaf !"

Time ticked. The engine lurked and wheezed -
Someone whimpered. Santa sneezed.
Then just before he reached his stop,
A gust of snowflakes fell - flip-flop...
The squeaky voice said: "We regret. Wrong sort of
snow. We'll beat it yet !"

A long while after, Santa stepped - Upon a platform.
Almost wept.
He trudged up hills at snail-rate
And found the forest track - TOO LATE !
He'd missed the runners. Missed the prize - His cup
of tea. His hot mince pies.

He stumbled back in wind and rain - To wait and
wait for one more train.
Home that night, with stress and strain,
He croaked: "I know I should complain...
But NEXT year - I'll avoid the fuss
And claim a FREE RIDE
On The Bus.

****

THE REPAIR SHOP.

****

Mrs. Claus had kept a secret -
For a month or two, but now
It was time for a confession,
But when ? Or where ? Or how ?
She flicked through T.V. channels -
Saw an Elf-Team take a bow.

A pair of merry Penguins -
Were mopping grateful eyes.
"You've made our Snowman smile again,"
They sniffed: "His hopes will rise...
Those twiggy feet and fingers mean -
He'll dance across the skies."

Then off they skipped and skidded -
With a jolly Christmas wave,
While Santa's Wife switched off the screen:
"Those Elves, I think could save
My sanity. My peace of mind.
But first I must be brave."

At once, she told the truth about -
Old Santa's Scruffy Bear !
She'd popped it in the washing
BUT
It shrunk...and lost its hair,
As well as ears and buttons -
Though it gained a one-eyed stare !

Of course, she'd tried to hide it:
"I loaned it to a friend,
Whose child was feeling needy."

But it drove her round the bend.
The time for LIES was over - She must find a
Happy End !

The Elves at the 'Repair Shop' - Were delighted to
be asked -
The Lady Elves went stitching,
While their Husbands, safely masked,
Were forming glassy eyeballs - And a GROWL !
The Spell was cast...

So Mrs. Claus took Santa - To The Shed Of
'Dreams-Come-True.'
He gazed in wonder at his Bear...
So fluffy. So brand new !
He hugged his Wife and blew his nose - As tissues
flapped and flew
While EVERYONE cried: "Hip Hooray !"

(The BEAR looked cheerful TOO !)

****

THE SPY IN THE SKY.
****

(A timely, cyber warning !)

Here is a warning - it's sad but true
Somebody, somewhere is studying YOU !
Someone who KNOWS when you're telling a lie,
Or starting a quarrel
And making friends cry.

Someone who SEES when you're spiteful.
Or mean.
Or when you're too lazy - to tidy or clean.
Someone who LISTENS and notes what you say -
The sharp words, the swear words,
That ruin a day.

Some one who NOTICES when you are kind -
Sharing and giving - or trying to find
Ways to make sorrow turn into a smile.
Ways to be helpful
Which CAN take a while.

But STILL you keep trying to do what is right.
And that's why, at Christmas, when day becomes
night...
And SOMEBODY jingles, up there on the roof,
(You might hear a laugh
Or the scrape of a hoof).

You'll know there is SOMEONE who looks at
His List,
Of people who should OR who shouldn't be missed.
He'll KNOW who's been nasty.
Or nice. Checks his sums -

And then it's too late
To be chewing your thumbs...
Even your Teachers ! Your Dads and your Mums !

For you'll never cheat
SANTA
When Christmas Eve comes.

****

THE WINTER-WORLD WORKERS.

****

I wonder how Santa and all his good friends
Fill up their time
When their Winter-Work ends ?

Well...
Rudolph's a Postman
Who hoofs down your street
To jingle your bell and deliver a treat.
The Gnomes in the Workshop
Build sheds for outside,
So Fathers and Husbands -
have somewhere to hide.

The Snowmen make mountains
Of ice-cream all day,
Then sleep in the fridge - so they won't melt away.
The Penguins are Waiters -
They're smart and they're willing.
They waddle at speed -
till their soup-bowls are spilling !

The Polar Bear teaches
Small cubs (with large towels)
To swim really quickly - as soon as she GROWLS.
The Fairy's a Super-Star
Hitting the heights
On a flying trapeze - in her shiny, pink tights.

The Elves are a Protest Group
Eager and keen
To save all our woodlands and shout:
"Let's Go Green !"

And as for Old Santa - It's no big surprise...
He's the Number One Taster
Of Merry Mince-Pies.
SO...
(Apart from a break at a beach in the West)
Santa and Company don't need a rest...
They're doing the jobs
That they ALL love the best.

****

Santa's
Pie Shop.

GOING FORWARD.

****

"EVERYONE says: "Going Forward,"
Groaned Santa. "But no one knows why !
Quite frankly, I'd rather go backwards
To times I recall with a sigh..."

"The evenings we sat by the fire
And we toasted our toes. Or we sang
In a group round the jolly piano -
Undisturbed, since the phone NEVER rang.
And NO ONE wrote e-mails at midnight,
Since no one had screens to be scanned;
Or mobiles demanding attention
ALL DAY - in the palm of your hand..."

"Of course," added kind Mother Christmas,
"You'd lose your new Sat-Nav as well,
And the carols you hear on your i-pod,
And the Microwave's jingly bell...
And the gizmo that stores T.V. programmes
When you fly round the World in one night -
And that Girl who can forecast a blizzard,
and the..."
"STOP !" whimpered Santa. "You're right !"

So they opened their Magical Laptop,
They checked on the Christmassy weather -
Then set off in warm, winter woollies
To try:
'Going Forward'
Together.

****

SNOW - GOGGLES.

****

The Snowmen slumped on sofas
In the comfy Reindeer Shed -
"Let's watch a jolly T.V. Show."
A bossy Snowgirl said.
So Frosty waved the gizmo
While the Reindeer clopped to bed.

The screen went slightly fizzy,
Then it cleared to show a crew
Of quite unlikely characters - Who watched the
T.V. too.
And made such silly comments
That the Snowmen shouted: "BOO !"

"Just look at that lot," Frosty fumed,
"They're worse than all the rest.
They chew and burp and tell rude jokes -
Their father's torn his vest !
And now they're chewing carrots...
That's a habit I detest."

But then, the Snowmen had to smile,
As funny Mrs. Posh
And Mister Posh drank classy wine -
And gasped and cried: "Oh gosh !
That other family's GHASTLY !
Do they EVER have a wash."

Our Snowfolk gazed and goggled
At the fools who showed no fear...
Who sat around in crazy clothes -
Who just had NO idea

That half the World was watching them
And grinning ear to ear !

But suddenly, a Snowchild asked:
"What IS that Gadget for ?
It's like an eyeball watching US...It swivels more
and more !"
That's when the Snow-Crowd all went pink,
And EVERYBODY swore !

They'll criticise the Silly Fools
On Goggle-Box
NO MORE !

****

WHAT'S IN A NAME.

****

(And At Last - An Audience Participation Puzzle...)

At Christmas - the Reindeer like quizzes and
Games -
So this year - their task is to:
'Guess The Right Names'.
And here come the Fairies, so flappy and sweet -
They twinkle and sing:
"Here's a LIST to complete !"

The Reindeer must say: 'Who is What ? It sounds
scary -
Choosing a Name for a fluttery Fairy.
But one of them winks and says: "Here's a small
clue:
Our Dad was called "NUFF -
The rest's up to you."

The First Fairy shivers. She sniffs and sounds gruff.
Then she sneezes on Blitzen
Who cries: "COLDY-NUFF."
The Second wears elegant, upper-class stuff.
She looks down on Prancer,
Who groans: "POSHY-NUFF."

The Third is a puzzle. She's fearsome. She's tough.
And what's more - she's HUGE !
Dancer laughs: "BIGGY-NUFF."
The Fourth Fairy's floppy. She looks a bit rough.
She YAWNS - until Comet
Says: "She's ADDY-NUFF !"

The Fifth is a Godmother. (Is that a bluff ?)

198

But she grants Donner's wish,
So he says: "GOODY-NUFF."
The Sixth Fairy's speedy, with plenty of puff...
She whizzes past Dasher
Who gasps: "FASTY-NUFF."

The Last is the Cutest. She's dressed in pink fluff -
So EVERYONE guesses -
Then shout: "SWEETY-NUFF."
The Contest is over. The hoofs scrape and scuff...
The Reindeer all wonder - Who's won ? And who's
Duff !
But the scores are a DRAW - So they shout:
"FAIRY-NUFF."

****

TWEET OF THE DAY.

****

There was a girl called Hash-Tag-Sue,
Who tapped her i-phone all day through,
At home, at work, at mealtimes too.
So, when her True-Love came along
She didn't think it rude or wrong
To text and twitter till...he'd GONE !

Her festive message said: "I'm fine.
Don't want romance - just gifts on-line.
And as for Christmas cards to sign...
You must be joking ! All I need
Is Broadband at the fastest speed,
Not lovey-dovey rhymes to read.

On Christmas Day, she thought she'd greet
The unknown friends she'd never meet,
With happy lies, inside a Tweet...
But in a flash, her plans back-fired -
The World-Wide-Web had just expired !
Her fingers shook. She felt unwired.

The room grew dark. A silence fell,
No cheery neighbours rang her bell,
No kindly voices broke the spell...
And as she sank in deep despair
A mocking chorus shook the air:
"You're lost. And no one seems to care !"

Of course, her nightmare WAS a dream.
She woke herself with one, wild scream...
And spied at once the magic gleam

200

Of morning stars. She heard the beat
Of muffled laughter, tip-toe feet,
Beyond her door and down the street.

She raised the latch. She gasped to see
A single parcel. One small tree -
'A Gift Of Love, To You, From Me.'

****

There is a girl called friendly Sue
Who taps her phone (as people do),
But speaks and smiles - and LISTENS too !
And though she often wonders who
Made every Christmas wish come true -
I think her True-Love knows.
Don't you ?
****

6. BOXING DAY AND AFTER !

BOXING DAY BLUES.

****

Everyone bored,
New toys ignored,
Who can afford
Boxing Day...

Batteries gone flat,
Torn paper-hat,
Feel cross and fat -
Boxing Day.

Crackers all gone,
Presents look wrong,
Too small, too long,
Boxing Day.

Tree starts to sag,
Time starts to drag,
Moan, fight and nag,
Boxing Day.

Gifts piled in mounds,
Jangling sounds,
Head throbs and pounds,
Boxing Day.

Cold food, cold plate,
Kitchen a state,
Who doesn't HATE
Boxing Day.

Games thrown on floor,
Wreath falls off door,
No patience - no more...
Boxing Day.

Ban it, I say !
Take it away.
It's over - hooray !
Boxing Day.

****

THE WAGES OF SIN.
****

The Penguins are safe in the Grotto,
Their blankets are fluffy and wide -
But who is that, lurking in shadows ?
Oh, who is that, coughing outside ?

The Reindeer are snug in their stables,
Their carrots are juicy and sweet -
But who is that, down by the dustbins ?
Oh, who is that, stamping his feet ?

The Elves are inside drinking cocoa,
They're swapping a seasonal joke -
But who is that, lost in a blizzard ?
Oh, who is that, starting to choke ?

Good gracious !
It's poor Father Christmas
Dreading his HUGE Yule-Log smoke.

****

AN OLFACTORY ODE.
****

Scents of Christmas come to me -
Wake a Childhood Memory...

The velvet aroma of ivy and pine;
Nan's winter dress with its soft, musty shine;
Seductive brown coils from the door of the kitchen;
Thick, spicy gravy and flakes of white chicken;
Stuffing that gushed in a great, herbal stream;
Bursts of fresh-air that were sharp, apple green;

Handfuls of talcum that clung for a day;
Satsuma segments to sparkle and spray;
A haze of hot slippers that steamed in the grate;
And hovering over us, certain as fate...
A circle of mist hid the tree and the star,
The spiralling fumes from
Dad's Christmas Cigar !

"My last," he would promise,
"I'll stop. Never fear."
And he did, I remember.
He
DID.
Every year !

****

EVERY YEAR.

****

Every year,
Just before Christmas,
They say...
"Rushed off our feet,
So much to do !
Don't know why we bother;
Can't seem to face it -
Can you ?"

And every year,
Just AFTER Christmas,
They say...
"Oh, very quiet you know,
Over so quickly too.
I don't know why we worried,
Can't think where it all went -
Can you ?

****

KEEP CALM AND CARRY ON.
****

When the gifts are too expensive,
When the bargains are a con,
When you start to scream at Santa -
Just keep calm - and carry on.

When the lights refuse to glitter,
When the only thing that shone
Was your nose in Winter Weather,
Just keep calm - and carry on.
When you're meant to bake a banquet
But your will to live has gone,
And the kitchen smells of burning,
Just keep calm - and carry on.

When the children drive you crackers,
When your eyes go wild and wan,
Then the puppy eats the tinsel -
Just keep calm - and carry on.
When your sister sails in smiling
Like a gorgeous, graceful swan
And you'd really like to scrag her -
Just keep calm - and carry on.

When you bulge inside your jumper
Like a mighty mastodon,
And you've eaten all the fruit-cake...
Just keep calm - and carry on.
When you're washing up and weepy
And you're feeling put upon,
And the bins are overflowing...
Just keep calm - and carry on.

When you're given Christmas kisses
By a dishy man called Don...
And you're scared you might be dreaming -
Hey !
Keep calm...
AND CARRY ON.

****

CHRISTMAS SHOPPING BLUES.
****

I've hunted for presents since August -
I've queued up for hours in the cold -
To get just what everyone wanted
Before all the bargains were sold.

I've thought and I've worried for ages
To make sure each gift was quite right...
So no one got smellies or tokens,
And none of the children would fight.

You'd think I'd be fed up with shopping,
You'd think I'd be happy to stop -
But even though Christmas is over,
Here I am, once again in the shop.

On my arm is a bagful of presents,
All for me
Out of Santa's big sack...
Awful colours, wrong sizes and useless,
SO
I'm taking the rotten lot back.

****

THANK YOU LETTERS.
****

As soon as the Big Day is over
There's something that HAS to be done -
A task that we all view with terror,
And no one could ever call fun.
We get out the paper and check-list,
Address book and stamps (second class);
Then sit - staring out of the window
At the scraps of mince pie on the grass.

We'd rather be clearing the gutters,
Or washing the car with a sponge,
Than trapped here indoors with a note-pad -
Too tongue-tied to tackle the plunge.
We'd rather be drying the dishes;
Or changing the sheets on the bed,
We'd even scrape fluff off the lamp-shades -
But here we sit, scratching our heads.

There's the pink, floral rug from an Aunty -
(Though the colour we asked for was Black).
There's the book with our names on the fly-leaf
So we can't take the wretched thing back.
There's the gadget that came from an Uncle
(We still can't decide what it's for);
There's the Calendar full of weird pictures
We've nailed to the back-bedroom door.

There's the token (again) from your brother,
Though we told him we'd much prefer cash;
There's a mountain of socks - cheap and cheerful,
That's bound to result in a rash;

There's the pottery dog from a sister
That leers in a sinister way -
No wonder we're biting our biros,
And can't think of ONE thing to say -

So we'll just have to hoover the bathroom,
Or clear out the junk from the shed -
And as for the letters - no thank you !
We'll write them tomorrow instead.

****

THANK YOU DOT CO DOT.
****

I USED to take ages on letters
Saying thank you for this and for that -
Jumpers that made me look awful,
Pilchards I gave to the cat...

But last year I hit on the answer -
A computerised message would do.
I'd just have to program the gizmo
And reel off a dozen or two.
So I sat down, quite keen and efficient,
To tap out a versatile note...
I shifted, deleted and centred,
I spell-checked (and saved) what I wrote.

I have to admit, it was tricky
To get all the sentiments right,
With phrases to suit every present,
While sounding sincere and polite.
I worked on the project each evening
Plus New Year and most weekends too -
I slaved over smart presentation,
Until there was no more to do.

The rest of the business was easy -
Just edit, then plug in the printer,
Inserting the name of the sender
Whose kindness had brightened my Winter.
Of course, there were one or two hitches,
(Since progress is not without stresses)
But by Easter, those letters were perfect...
And I just had to load the addresses.

In fact - the results were a triumph.
I don't for one moment regret it...
BUT
This year I'm buying a biro
And as for computers -
FORGET IT !

****

THE OFFICE PARTY POEM.

****

I'm here at the annual Party -
A tradition that has to be faced;
Though the jokes and the seasonal costumes
Are all in the very worst taste.

I carry my Self-Defence Manual
(No mistletoe nonsense for me)
And as for that Rep with the ear-ring:
I've told him I'm simply not free.

No furtive romance in the print-room,
The store cupboard's strictly taboo -
And if anyone tries to harass me
They'll see what this holly can do !

So no one's attempted to squeeze me,
Or offer me too much to drink -
Nobody's cuddled or teased me,
Or aimed me a nudge or a wink !

No one's made saucy suggestions,
Or sexist remarks from the floor,
In fact
It's been quite inoffensive...

I'm not coming here any more !

****

PARTY PROBLEM.

****

I was asked to a party - but what could I wear ?
I trudged round the shops in a state of despair...
Since all the new styles
Were too weird. Or too small.
Too pink. Or too pricey. Or - not right at all.

And most of the dresses - I'll sound like a prude,
Were saucy and see-through and draughty and RUDE !
The whole expedition
Was hurting my brain.
Should I try one more store ? Should I jump on the
train ?
WELL...
I went to the party - so what did I choose ?
A sleek, slinky number in dazzling blues -
With a matching silk jacket
And sex-goddess shoes,
And nobody else had an outfit like mine,
So classy. So retro. So simply divine !

My friends gazed in envy - admired every stitch.
Decided I must be disgustingly rich !
They longed for my secret,
I just tapped my lip -
But I'll tell it to you if you don't let it slip !

My chic Vintage clothes - didn't make my jaw drop...
I found the whole lot
In our Charity Shop.

****

(For our local Charity Shops !)

GIVE US A KISS.
****

I hurried along to the market - the weather was
crisp with desire,
I sorted through boxes of fir-cones and holly with
berries of fire...
Until I found just what I wanted,
Seductively spread on the stall -
Resplendent with branches of promise - a mistletoe
bough for the hall.

I hung it with care and with passion - silver thread
looped around a gold pin -
My paper hat shook with emotion - Now the fun was
about to begin.

The first to arrive was an Aunty - With lipstick that
tasted of soap;
The next was a girl from the office - who gave me a
peck, but no hope.
The third was a feminist actress
Who called me embarrassing names;
The fourth was a woman in slippers - who said she
was too old for games.

The fifth was a rather small cousin - who giggled
and pulled off my hat;
The sixth was engaged to my brother - so THAT, as
she told me, was that.
The seventh was charming but icy;
The eighth had a cold in her head;
The ninth was just selling insurance - so I poured
her a cocoa instead.

The tenth was a real Christmas cracker - just my
type, just my height, just my style;
My paper crown started to quiver - as I gave her my
'Step-This-Way' smile;
She kissed all my brothers and uncles;
The boys from the club - one by one;
She kissed a young lad who had acne - she even
kissed Grandad for fun !

She kissed our new vicar (politely) - plus anyone
else she could see...
In fact, she used up every berry - so there wasn't
one twig left for me !
I stood there, alone for a moment,
Dejected and weary of life...
Then I found just the person I wanted -
And gave a BIG kiss
To my Wife.

****

Now - it's Pantomime Time.
Oh no it isn't - Oh yes it is...

PANTOMIME TIME.
****

CHORUS:
At last, it's joke and laughter time,
It's happy-ever-after time - for hearing tales in
songs and rhyme,
With people from the Pantomime !

(Chorus)

CINDERELLA.
They call me Cinderella - and I sit alone at nights,
Which means I won't be marrying - a Prince in
purple tights.
But though my clothes are tattered - and my sisters
ugly gluttons...
Forget about those crystal shoes...
I'd rather marry Buttons.

(Chorus)

UGLY SISTER.
Although I wear a skirt and wig - you all know I'm a
fellah !
I play an Ugly Sister so - that's why I'm called
Rubella.
No wonder I'm so spiteful - and as bad as rotten
eggs...
I'm wearing saggy, baggy tights
To match my wrinkled legs !

219

(Chorus)

WICKED WITCH.
Don't BOO ! Or call me nasty - 'Cos I'm really kind
and good...
I'll prove it if you step inside - my cottage in the
wood.
So when I give you lollipops - or gingerbread that's
HOT,
And tell you I'm a sweetie...
Please don't shout:
"Oh No You're Not !"

(Chorus)

DICK WHITTINGTON.
Dick Whittington they call me - I trudge to London
Town;
I'm forced to act with animals - Which really gets
me down !
I sing, I dance, I hear Bow Bells - I wear a fancy
hat...
But all the children want to see
Is just my stupid CAT.

(Chorus)

Continued...

2.
(More Pantomime Characters.)

CAPTAIN HOOK.
You must remember Captain Hook - who led the
Pirate Band,
And bravely fought with Peter Pan - in Never-Never
Land...
But still I'm always terrified - the Crocodile will find
me -
So every time I walk on stage,
I have to:
'Look Behind Me !'

(Chorus.)

ALADDIN.
Hello ! It's me - Aladdin - and though I'm quite a
rascal,
With luck I'll win a Princess - and a magic, flying
castle.
I have a rotten Uncle, but - I'm not afraid of
Meanies,
I've got my rings, my magic lamp
And my designer Genies.

(Chorus)

DAISY THE COW.
I'm everybody's favourite - because I raise a
laugh...
Although tonight I've come along - without my
UDDER half !
You like it when I'm waltzing - and my bucket slowly
spins
But most of all - you love it when
My milk comes out in tins !

(And finally...)

At last it's joke and laughter time -
It's 'Happy-Ever-After' time;
For hearing tales in song and rhyme
With people from the
PANTOMIME !

****

A MOO-VING TALE.

****

I am Daisy the Cow,
I've perfected my bow,
I can HOOF round the stage like a star.
I've projected my MOO
For an entrance and cue -
So I'm HERD in the Stalls - and the Bar.

When I waggle my ears
There are rapturous cheers,
And I MILK every MOOVE for a laugh,
Yet there's one thing I lack
Which is holding me back...
I'm a HEIFER with no UDDER half.

So I do things in halves,
With a cramp in my CALVES -
Just to prove I can still be aMOOsing...
But I'm semi-detached
And my act has been scrapped
Since a two-legged COW is confusing !

Now my Rear-View reminds me
My future's BEHIND-ME,
I'm put out to grass and forgotten...
While my tragical TAIL,
Like a leaky old pail,
Has to END...MOOvingly...
At ROCK-BOTTOM.

****

(MOO whenever MOOved.)

223

THE CHRISTMAS GROTTO GAMES.

****

(Spoken by an enthusiastic but
breathless Sports-Reporter.)

"And...
They're all lining up for the Grand Final -
Santa is testing his new, spiky boots,
(Plain black as usual - ideal for steep chimneys).
The Gnomes are still puffing
After a training run with the Polar Bear;
The Snowmen are adjusting their noses
(No wobbly carrots allowed)...
And the Safety Elves are searching the Reindeer
For Go-Faster Spells.

Meanwhile, the Penguins are warming-up
With a spot of egg-juggling;
Rudolph is flashing his nose (which CAN'T be legal)
And the Grotto Elf - wearing soggy, green slippers,
Doesn't have a hope.

The last few contestants are arriving, just in time !
The Fairy's at the top of her tree,
She's waving her wand - and they're OFF !

The Penguins have fallen at the first fence,
The Chief Snowman has tripped over his own scarf,
And the Elf (as expected) has limped back to bed...
But the Gnomes, running in relays,
Have whizzed round the Igloo
And overtaken Prancer and Dancer
(Who probably ate too many mince pies.)

Now here comes the Polar Bear,
looking dangerous -
He's already crossed the Glacier in record time
And he's only just behind Rudolph
Who is simply flying along.
It's neck and antler -
Only Old Santa Claus can beat them now...

They've reached the last obstacle
(A rather tempting stocking entirely filled with
sweets).
The Gnomes can't resist,
Rudolph and Santa are sharing the toffees -
And the Bear is chewing a chocolate mouse...

But wait !
Who is this, clopping past the pack
And clanging her bell ?
Is it ?
Can it be ?
YESSSSS !

It's Daisy the Pantomime Cow
Winning Santa's Sack of Super Surprises -
And that, my friends -
Is what I call
An Udderly Happy Ending.

****

(Now - back to some sort of reality...)

THE LAST DAY OF CHRISTMAS.

****

Throw away the mistletoe,
The tinsel and the holly..
It's too late now for paper-chains,
It's too late to be jolly.

Sweep away each silver star,
Each needle and each berry,
It's too late now for fairy-lights -
It's too late to be merry.

Clear away the Christmas cards -
Come on ! Make it snappy...
It's too late now for party hats,
It's too late to be happy.

For Christmas is over,
There's no more good cheer -
So we can be gloomy -
At least
Till next year !

****

(Look out - the BONGS are ready...)

BONG !
****

BONG ! And now the Midnight News is
booming round the room.
And
BONG ! The Reader's weighty words are
warning us of doom...
And every sort of ghastliness -
and grief and greed and gloom.

And BONG ! Our man in Foreign Parts is
speaking with a sigh.
And BONG ! An evil virus soon will tumble
from the sky...
So if we're feeling fine today -
tomorrow we could die.

And BONG ! Here comes the Weather Girl,
who points at stormy seas.
And BONG ! We'll either boil to death,
or drown in floods - or freeze;
Or wicked winds will sweep away our houses and
our trees.

And BONG ! Let's hear a Local Tale of
misery and woe.
And BONG ! A brand new road will run where
flowers used to grow.
And here's another angry crowd with sticks and
bricks to throw !
And:
BONG !
Switch off the rotten News.
Find something else to say -

The World is full of Kindness too. And Love. And
Joy. Hooray !
The starlight glows. The children dream.
And here's a brand new day.

****

THE WINTER RITUAL.

****

(Look out for this seasonal ceremony -
next time you are in a public space.)

All the people bow their heads
As if they are at prayer.

All the people mutter words
That float on frosty air.

All the people concentrate
And lick their chilly lips...

And all because
They CAN'T do up
Their stupid winter
ZIPS.

****

(Good luck.)

(Then Covid came along ! So this was the year
when we saw
our friends and families on ZOOM.)

ZOOM.
****

(Christmas 2020.)

A virtual Christmas is looming,
The Virus can't ruin our day...
We've all cracked the code - so we're Zooming !
And we're dressed in our best.
Hip-hooray.

But:
Gran has got stuck in a corner,
And Grandad is stopping on Mute -
And we all look incredibly ancient...
What happened ?
We used to be cute.

Dad, in his Santa Claus jumper
Has hung decorations with care;
While Mum's found some old Christmas photos -
The magic we all love to share.

Then Aunty admits she's been cheating -
Her top-half is terribly smart,
But under the table - she's wearing
Odd socks that are falling apart.

Our Cousins will grumble for ages -
There's the Lock-Down, the ruined career...
But the Children will plunder a Joke Book
To brighten this long, lonely year.

NOW:

Our forty-five minutes are over,
Our farewells have come from the heart,
And we wish we could hug one another -
As the screen
Softly tears us apart.

Yet somehow, we seem to be smiling...
Our memories keep us all warm -
So we'll grab a great handful of courage
And together
We'll face every storm.

****

(Poor old Rudolph was upset - because he had to
wear a mask.)

RUDOLPH'S 2020 RANT.

****

Rudolph's in a dreadful mood -
He's off his friends, he's off his food -
He spends his day
Just kicking hay !
His language, frankly, can be rude.

The other Reindeer whizz - and wear
Their masks without a single care.
In fact - they're warm
In snow and storm,
As well as beating germs. So there !

At last, Old Santa went to see
Why Rudolph ranted: "Look at Me !
This ghastly thing
Tied on with string,
Has stolen my identity."

"My life is wrecked. I've lost my pride.
I'm ruined," Rudolph sniffed and sighed.
"My nose can't glow,
Can't guide you so...
I'm USELESS now," the poor Deer cried.

BUT

Santa (with his Elves and Co.)
Said: "Cheer up Rudolph. Off we go !
You'll lead our sleigh
Your bright-light way...
We don't need masks outside you know !"

While Snowmen yelled:
"WE TOLD YOU SO !"

****

7. GOOD INTENTIONS.

BRAVE FACES.
****

Christmas makes Heroes of us all...

The Givers, who hand over their own hopes,
And good intentions
Without flinching.

The Takers, who gasp with pleasure
At kindly disasters,
Loving disappointments.

The Hosts, who bustle through steam
And crumpled paper,
Beaming like actors in a Victorian Play.

The Visitors, who admire and praise
And never say:
"But this is not the true, the proper way."

The Private Souls,
Who tuck their precious solitudes
Inside small pockets of peace.

The Impatient Ones,
Who hide their spiky tempers
Behind smiles as bright candle flames.

The Noisy Ones, who bite their lips
And tiptoe softly around sleeping babies,
Snoring elders.

The Little Ones, who somehow decipher
Unwritten rules,
And squeal with delight at every, unfathomable
surprise.

The Stay-At-Homes, who willingly
Scrape ice from car windows,
And dive into the dark with parcels of joy.

The Wanderers, trapped in deep chairs,
Where whirling rooms spin
Like childhood memories.

The Cool Characters,
Who briefly, bravely
Wear Cracker hats and hopeless jumpers.

The Lonely Ones,
Who strain to hear faint voices
From far away.
Who trail tinsel around old photographs
And hide their sadness
In a secret drawer.

And Everyone who chooses
(Despite the lost Yesterdays,
The unknown Tomorrows)
To wrap this one magical day
In a warm cloak of happiness.

Christmas Makes Heroes
Of Us All.

****

THE HERO.
****

(A poem in honour of Captain Sir Tom Moore -
who raised money for our N.H.S.)

When you are old - when tales are told
Of Heroes brave and proud -
You'll pause a while - then simply smile
And call one name out loud.

You'll hurry past - the famous cast
Of cartoon Super Stars,
With mighty fists - with magic gifts
And weapons sent from Mars !

For YOU have seen - On-line, on screen,
A man who scoffed at pain;
Who would not fail - to trudge his trail
Each day ! Again...again...

Quite soon, he knew - a fortune grew
To help in times of need -
Yet still he stepped - as funding leapt
To honour man and deed.

You stood to clap - his final lap,
One hundred days...and years !
You watched with pride - the man who tried
To comfort all our fears.

At last, you'll pay - your own: "Hooray !"
To one who hated war.
Who walked to show - How love can grow:
Our Captain
Sir Tom Moore.

****

(1920 - 2021.)

THE KINDLY MAGICIANS.
****

(For all our dear, absent friends.)

Some people are Christmassy
All the year through.
Their mouths are designed for smiles.
Their voices are as rich as plum puddings.
Their eyes are always ready to sparkle like stars.

When they walk into a room,
Even strangers relax
And lean back in their comfy chairs,
Knowing that the air will soon fizz
With gentle fun -
And friendly words will be handed out
Like gifts
For everyone.

And when these kindly magicians
Turn to go -
Waving in their usual Christmassy way,
The warmth they leave behind them
Seems to stay.

****

THE MAGIC OF CHRISTMAS.

****

The Magic has gone -
That's what they say.
It's not the same as
In my young day.

There's too much expense,
Too much fretting -
Not enough giving,
And too much getting.

But as for myself -
I just can't wait
To put a mince pie
On Santa's plate...

To hang up my socks,
And write my list -
To wake at dawn
Well...
You get the gist.

So don't tell me
The Magic has flown -
I'll close my eyes
And
I'll find my own.

****

WRITER'S BLOCK.
****

(Because everyone gets stuck sometimes...)

I'm trying to think of a Seasonal Sermon,
With masses of morals
For people to squirm on.

I'm trying to find a traditional text
That won't give away what I plan to write next.
An Advent dilemma I suffer each year
As soon as the Sunday School Angels appear.

I try to be novel - as far as I'm able,
But I've said all I can, about beasts in a stable.
I've done all that stuff about NOT being greedy
And sharing your feast with the poor and the needy.

It has to be festive without seeming funny -
In case they're too merry to leave any money !
My Christmas Day homily must be a good one,
To keep all their minds off the food in the oven.

It can't be too brisk, but it mustn't be boring...
Or parents will doze and they'll all end up snoring.
The children will fidget if things get too solemn -
They'll test their new toys round the back of the
column.

So I sit here and hope for divine inspiration...
To please every pew in the whole congregation.
My brain is a blank and my pen's gone all jerky !
My head's full of shepherds - with gifts of roast
turkey...

It's now Christmas Eve - and I couldn't feel sicker...
I must have been crazy
To marry a Vicar !

****

OH NO ! NOT MORE FAKE NEWS !
****

This Christmas, all our dreams came true !
Our day together simply flew -
Our gifts and feasts were perfect too.

And as the Old Year drifts away,
The Future glows. I'm here to say:
Our happy Nation cries: "Hooray."

Our N.H.S. is safe at last -
It's richly funded, fears have passed,
So operations happen fast.

Our schools are full of shining faces;
Cheerful teachers; welcome spaces;
New equipment, - progress races !

And look ! A mass of Money Trees...
Cash for kids and O.A.P's.
Homes that never boil. Nor freeze.

No more Food Banks ! No more gloom...
Rents are cheap and High Streets boom;
Buses run and railways zoom.

People LIKE each other more.
Pollution's gone. We've closed that door -
Our air is cleaner than before.

****

But wait !
Oh dear...I start to shake,
My dream is over. I'm awake -
Forgive me for my mad mistake.

All hopes are dashed - I'm full of dread
An awful future lies ahead...
I think I'll just go back
To bed.

****

RING OUT THE OLD.

****

(I first wrote this poem in 1991.
I keep waiting for it to go out of date !)

"What did you do ?"
The New Year said.
The Old Year hung his weary head...

****

"What did I do - and what have I done ?
Of all my dreams, survives there none ?"

"I promised to fill the Earth with joy,
Yet still the fires of greed destroy."

"I promised to rid the World of hate -
Yet still the bullets cry: 'Too Late !'"

"I promised to set the innocent free -
Yet still they shake their chains at me."

"I promised to dry the children's tears -
Yet still their nights are chilled with fears."

"I promised to cleanse the hungry lands,
Yet still they beg with bony hands."

"I promised to bring equality -
Must all my wishes die with me ?"

****

The Old Year hung his guilty head...
"But it's my turn now,"
The New Year said.

****

THE CLOTHES OF CHRISTMAS.
****

Cast off your Cloak of Anger,
Your tangled Scarf of Care.
Undo your Busy Buttons,
The Boots of Gloom you wear.

Put on your Rainbow Jumper,
Your Happy Paper-Crown.
A pair of Joyful Slippers
To lead you through the town.

Then share a Coat of Kindness
With the lonely and the poor...
And stitch their torn and tattered dreams,
With Threads of Hope once more.

****

THE WORLD IS TOO MUCH WITH US.

****

(With apologies to Wordsworth.)

When the News gets us down,
When we fret and we frown,
And the World's in a terrible mess -
So the outlook seems bleak
As the scientists speak
Of a future designed for distress.

When we can't find a spark
That will banish the dark
And the gloom is an unending trial -
We can curl up and sigh
As the days stumble by
Or fight our despair with a smile.

We can cheerfully greet
All the strangers we meet;
We can offer to help an old friend.
Then with luck we can start
A change of the heart
When our kindness becomes a new trend.

We can't (on our own)
Roll a burden of stone
But together, perhaps we can find
The pathways of peace
Which will softly increase,
To lead through a maze of the mind.

SO

Let enmity die
As we shake hands and try
To conquer our anger and pride...
Then, perhaps the New Year
Will bring hope - and good cheer
As we set all our problems aside.

****

GOOD INTENTIONS.
****

Now, we've all made Resolutions
At the start of each New Year...
We've tried to shake the habits that refuse to
disappear,
The sweets. The treats. The spending
On the stuff we think we need.
The time we waste on gadgets - plus the gossiping
and greed.

But this year, we've discovered
We are kinder than we thought !
We've helped our friends and neighbours - We've
hoped that no one caught
The shadow of the Virus
Which has turned our routines round.
We've filled our streets with rainbows - We have
listened. We have found...

The music of a songbird;
The perfume of a flower.
The joy we felt when walking
Through a woodland for an hour.
The rosy streaks of sunset.
The cobwebs strung with light.
The buzz of bees in hedgerows.
The winter's starry night.

And though we've groaned and grumbled
While the whole World seemed to sigh...
We've carried on. We've done our best
To beat the blues. That's why...

When all our fears have faded
And our normal lives begin -
Remember Nature. Friendship.
Love.
And let our Best Selves
WIN.

****

THE SUPER STARS.

****

Some stars seem fixed forever,
Their light shines on and on -
Until, one day they vanish
And we can't believe they've gone.

We've waved good bye to many names,
Those characters from Soaps;
Or childhood heart-throbs; heroes who
Inspired our secret hopes.

And now Sir Ken has left us
For a shiny, new address -
So when he meets an Angel
Who is showing signs of stress,
He'll wave his tickling stick to spread
The Gift Of Happiness.

And you'll remember other Stars,
Whose light was strong and true -
They scattered love and comfort when
Your whole world tipped askew...

But if you close your eyes and wish,
They'll shine again
For you.

****

And Finally...
A WISH LIST.
****

What would I wish
(If wishes came true)
For Christmas Day
For each of you ?

The Gift of Happiness - Precious and rare.
Half for yourself,
And half to share.

And laughter, of course - The sort that is kind -
It's hidden away
But it's easy to find.

Then a Coat of Courage - To keep you warm
Through the darkest night
And the wildest storm.

A Packet of Patience - To save and to play
On the lonely voyage,
The tedious day.

A Key of Good Luck - To open the Gate
Of the long-lost Garden,
The Pathway of Fate.

And last -
A gift deceptively small,
(It can blaze like a comet;
Or shatter a wall;

Or hold you close
Whenever you call)
A Casket of Love
For you all,

For You All.

****

ABOUT THE AUTHOR.

Clare Bevan used to be a teacher, and she still loves visiting schools. Her first book won the Kathleen Fiddler Award, which was a wonderful thrill. Now she is best known for her children's poetry - and her poems can be found in over one hundred anthologies.

More recently, she became Bracknell's First Poet Laureate, and her favourite poem was about the women who flew the Spitfires in World War Two.

Clare lives in a cobwebby house (since she likes spiders), and her husband keeps her sane when she's scared of computers.

Her hobbies are: performing her poems; wearing hats; feeding the birds in her garden, and riding a big, purple tricycle !

And of course - she loves Christmas.